PUBLICATIONS IN LIBRARIANSHIP NO. 67

Assessing Liaison Librarians: Documenting Impact for Positive Change

Edited by Daniel C. Mack and Gary W. White

Association of College and Research Libraries
A division of the American Library Association
Chicago, Illinois 2014

The paper used in this publication meets the minimum requirements of American National Standard for Information Sciences–Permanence of Paper for Printed Library Materials, ANSI Z39.48-1992. ∞

Library of Congress Cataloging-in-Publication Data

Assessing liaison librarians : documenting impact for positive change / edited by Daniel C. Mack and Gary W. White.
    pages cm. -- (Publications in librarianship ; #67)
    Includes bibliographical references.
    ISBN 978-0-8389-8708-7 (pbk.) -- ISBN 978-0-8389-8709-4 (pdf) -- ISBN 978-0-8389-8710-0 (epub) -- ISBN 978-0-8389-8711-7 (kindle) 1. Academic libraries--Evaluation. 2. Academic libraries--Relations with faculty and curriculum. 3. Academic librarians--Professional relation-ships. 4. Academic librarians--Rating of. 5. Research--Methodology--Study and teaching (Higher) 6. Communication in learning and schol-arship--Technological innovations. 7. Libraries and colleges--United States--Case studies. 8. Academic libraries--United States--Case studies. 9. Research libraries--United States--Case studies. I. Mack, Daniel C., editor. II. White, Gary W., editor.
    Z675.U5A5977 2014
    027.7--dc23
                            2014041523

Printed in the United States of America.

18 17 16 15 14 5 4 3 2 1

Contents

Introduction
Libraries and Assessment

Daniel C. Mack
Associate Dean for Collection Strategies and Services
University of Maryland Libraries
College Park, MD

Gary W. White, PHD
Associate Dean for Public Services
University of Maryland Libraries
College Park, MD

Like any other constituency of the academic community, librarians understand that assessment is an increasingly important topic in the twenty-first-century university. While some librarians are familiar with assessment, to many it is at best only vaguely understood. Some consider it just a trendy buzzword, while others believe that it applies only to specific programs and activities, such as bibliographic instruction and targeting of serials for cancelation. The truth is that assessment is neither a passing trend nor a limited activity. Rather, assessment will continue to be integrated into all areas of practice in academia, including the research library. Nearly all librarians will be involved in assessment activities to some degree. This includes librarians who serve as liaisons to academic departments, disciplinary researchers, and other specific audiences.

Unfortunately, many librarians not only are unfamiliar with assessment in general, but also do not understand how it relates to their work as liaison librarians or how it can assist them in improving the services they offer. To incorporate assessment in the activities of liaison librarians, the institution must first have a focused vision of the role of liaisons within

1

the academy. By identifying the various roles that liaisons play, including reference and research consultant, instruction librarian, collection developer, and other responsibilities, the library can then ascertain specific tasks that liaisons perform in each of these capacities. This process can then lead to establishing assessment measures and creating assessment tools to evaluate performance and document the impact that liaisons have on the library, the university, and the user communities that they serve.

This book offers liaison librarians and those who supervise them specific guidance on how to incorporate assessment into their work. In order to establish a working definition of *assessment* and its importance in higher education, the work starts with White's overview of the role of assessment in the contemporary academy and how this role affects liaison librarians. Because most liaison librarians spend a significant portion of their time assisting users in identifying relevant information resources, Murphy and Gibson present a model for assessment of research services. Bibliographic and other library instruction continues to be a key component of liaison librarians' efforts, which Cahoy addresses by focusing on assessment activities related to teaching, learning, and literacies. In many libraries, liaison librarians increasingly offer support for online, distance, and other nontraditional learning. Barefoot offers advice on how assessment of liaison activities in online and blending learning can become part of an overall assessment program. Addressing the rapidly changing topic of library collections and information resources, Mack demonstrates that assessment of collection development must now expand beyond examination of collections and also document how collection development activities are integrated into the intellectual life of the institution. Scholarly communication continues to play an important part in academic libraries' overall suite of services, and Childress and Hickey discuss the role of assessment in these endeavors. Examining a broad vision of liaison librarians' relationships with academic departments, the university, and other researchers, Bidney presents the central place of assessment in engagement and outreach to the academic community. Professional development is vital to any successful liaison program, and a robust assessment program can target activities and areas of responsibility that require additional training. White addresses the importance of ongoing training in his recommendations for creating a professional development program for liaison librarians. The work concludes with Mack's advice for designing and implementing a liaison assessment program that is relevant to the specific needs of individual libraries and librarians.

The twenty-first-century academic library requires an ongoing, proactive, and relevant program of assessment for its liaison librarians. The outcomes of such a program will ensure that the library's suite of services remains central to the teaching mission and research enterprise of the university. Properly conducted and incorporated into a professional development program, assessment can transform good librarians into great librarians.

Chapter One

The Place of Liaisons and the Central Role of Assessment in American Higher Education

Gary W. White, **PHD**

Associate Dean for Public Services
University of Maryland Libraries
College Park, MD

Introduction

Assessment is a core practice in higher education and one that has become increasingly important over the past decade as external pressures for accountability have grown. Articles questioning the quality and affordability of higher education appear regularly in both the popular press and the professional literature for higher education. Clearly, assessment has become an important issue for anyone involved in higher education administration. This trend for more extensive assessment is also impacting academic libraries. Likewise, there is a plethora of professional literature on how libraries can conduct assessment activities and demonstrate their value within the academy. This chapter provides an overview of assessment within the twenty-first-century research library and the important role that liaisons play in library assessment programs.

Before discussing assessment and how it pertains to libraries and liaisons, it is important to first define what we mean by *assessment*. Broadly speaking, *assessment* refers to "the gathering of information concerning the functioning of students, staff, and institutions of higher education.

The basic motive for gathering it is to improve the functioning of the institution and its people."[1] The National Academy for Academic Leadership provides an excellent overview of assessment principles as they relate to higher education, and it is worthwhile to cover these principles briefly in order to provide context for this book. According to the National Academy, one needs to distinguish between assessment and evaluation:

> **Assessment** is a process of determining "what is." Assessment provides faculty members, administrators, trustees, and others with evidence, numerical or otherwise, from which they can develop useful information about their students, institutions, programs, and courses and also about themselves. This information can help them make effectual decisions about student learning and development, professional effectiveness, and program quality. **Evaluation** uses information based on the credible evidence generated through assessment to make judgments of relative value; the acceptability of the conditions described through assessment.[2]

Astin and Antonio categorize these two as different but related activities. According to them, assessment can be the gathering of information (measurement) and the use of that information for institutional and individual improvement (evaluation).[3]

The National Academy also defines three types of assessment:

- **Outcomes:** "the ultimate results desired or actually achieved."
- **Processes:** "the programs, services and activities developed to produce the desired outcomes."

- **Inputs:** resources, including faculty, staff, and students, finances, and facilities and other physical resources. Inputs also include the "psychological climate" for assessment.[4]

While outcomes assessment provides information on the results, process assessments are necessary in order to determine why the results were achieved. Outcomes assessment alone is therefore not sufficient. Input assessments are important because they help us to understand our institutions as well as providing assistance in designing programs and services.

Assessment in Higher Education

Assessment has received significant attention and has triggered debate in the higher education community. Assessment, whether driven by genuine desire to improve teaching and learning, by mandates, or by the need to satisfy accreditors, legislators, and the public, is a complex endeavor that has spawned literally thousands of articles, monographs, and reports. This section will provide a cursory overview of assessment as it pertains to higher education.

Generally, assessment in higher education has three broad purposes:

- to certify individual student achievement
- to improve programs
- to hold higher education accountable to its constituents[5]

However, assessment can take place for a wide variety of specific purposes, including measuring student learning, providing feedback to students about progress and how they can improve learning, providing teachers with information about their teaching effectiveness, determining student progression toward program or degree qualifications, and providing feedback and information to an institution about the quality of its programs and its support of faculty and students in these programs.[6] Research on assessment in higher education is abundant, covering such areas as learner-centered assessment, program assessments, and issues to related to faculty perceptions and acceptance of assessment.[7]

There are a wide variety of ways to conduct assessment, far beyond what is possible to discuss in this introductory chapter, but it is important to understand why we assess and also to understand some general best practices. The American Association for Higher Education has concluded that there are nine core principles for good practice in conducting assessments:

1. **The assessment of student learning begins with educational value.** Assessment is not an end in itself but a vehicle for educational improvement....

2. **Assessment is most effective when it reflects an understanding of learning as multidimensional, integrated, and revealed in performance over time....**

3. **Assessment works best when the programs it seeks to improve have clear, explicitly stated purposes....**

4. **Assessment requires attention to outcomes but also and equally to the experiences that lead to those outcomes....**

5. **Assessment works best when it is ongoing not episodic....**

6. **Assessment fosters wider improvement when representatives from across the educational community are involved....**

7. **Assessment makes a difference when it begins with issues of use and illuminates questions that people really care about....**

8. **Assessment is most likely to lead to improvement when it is part of a larger set of conditions that promote change....**
9. **Through assessment, educators meet responsibilities to students and to the public.**[8]

As implied above, the reasons for conducting assessment must be articulated and accepted if assessment practices are to be embraced by faculty and others. Havens notes that assessment has become a "divisive force" at many colleges and universities for several reasons.[9] These include pressures to conduct assessment activities quickly, such as meeting accreditation deadlines; focus on the process instead of on making improvements; worries about loosening requirements in order to boost performance; workload issues; and the impact on adjuncts or others who may not be part of the planning and decision-making processes. These are issues that academic libraries must also consider when designing and developing programs of assessment. It is clear that institutions of higher education are facing increased environmental pressures to conduct assessments and to demonstrate learning, value, and accountability.

Assessment in Academic Libraries

At the same time that there has been significant growth in attention to assessment in higher education, academic libraries have been increasingly engaged in assessment activities. While some tools such as LibQUAL have been used for quite some time,[10] in the past decade there have been accelerated efforts to demonstrate that libraries contribute to student learning outcomes.[11] In addition, as with all parts of higher education, libraries are increasingly called upon to demonstrate their "value" in supporting research, teaching, and learning. Various studies and projects, such as the Association of College and Research Libraries' *Value of Academic Libraries: A Comprehensive Research Review and Report* and the Association of Research Libraries' Library Assessment Conference, currently held every two years, focus on methods that libraries can use to assess their contributions to higher education.[12]

Demonstrating the value and assessing impact of academic libraries is particularly difficult, as much of the literature discusses. Libraries are challenged with demonstrating their own value in an era when perceptions of the necessity of libraries are changing and there are increased calls for accountability for investments in resources. The Association of Research Libraries has taken a lead role in this area, sponsoring conferences focusing on assessment and providing other resources and initiatives to highlight the need for assessment. According to Kyrillidou and Jaggers, recent themes of these assessment conferences include focus on library outcomes related to research, faculty productivity, and student performance.[13] They do note that this is an emerging area of study and that most of these activities are still in the research and development phases. Being able to demonstrate this value is the underlying purpose of this book.

Academic libraries use assessment activities to measure and evaluate a wide variety of library services and functions. Hufford provides a comprehensive overview of the research and literature on library assessment during the past decade.[14] His article outlines the major research conducted and published in the areas of library administration, collections, and public services, among other areas. There are a wide variety of research studies regarding assessment in areas such as journal collections, special collections, e-books, discovery tools and systems, web pages, instructional and information literacy programs, support of distance education, reference and research services, interlibrary loan, and library spaces and learning commons.[15]

Academic libraries are also recognizing the importance of creating and sustaining a culture of assessment within their organizations. As noted above, faculty can be reluctant to embrace assessment activities, and there are often concerns about the reasons for and methods of conducting assessment. Libraries are in a similar situation where librarians may not fully understand or embrace the need or techniques for assessment. As

Farkas notes, some view assessment as "mechanistic," i.e., something they must do because it is required.[16] For others, assessment may go against beliefs in academic freedom and independence of professionals. As a result, there is a growing body of literature on how to create a "culture of assessment" in academic libraries. *Organizational culture* refers to the beliefs and values held and understood by members of an organization, as well as the practices and behaviors of these members. In other words, it is a "shared mental model" that members of an organization hold.[17] According to Lakos and Phipps, a "culture of assessment" is

> an organizational environment in which decisions are based on facts, research, and analysis, and where services are planned and delivered in ways that maximize positive outcomes and impacts for customers and stakeholders. A culture of assessment exists in organizations where staff care to know what results they produce and how those results relate to customers' expectations. Organizational mission, values, structures, and systems support behavior that is performance and learning focused.[18]

However, creating a culture of assessment, as with any organizational change, is challenging and requires strong leadership. Both Lakos and Phipps and Farkas discuss strategies for transforming the organizational culture of libraries into a "culture of assessment."[19] Chapter 8 in this book, on professional development, suggests ways that libraries can support the assessment of liaison activities from an organizational perspective, thus emphasizing the importance of assessment from organizational leadership.

Purpose of This Book

The concept for this book arose when the editors were discussing the role of the research library in today's research universities with a group of nonlibrarian research and teaching faculty. While there was agreement that the words *library* and *librarian* continue to evoke mental schemas of physical buildings and print materials even in this era of digitization and ubiquitous access, the group agreed that the fundamental functions of librarians and libraries really have not changed—our overarching goal is providing access to information. In research libraries, it is primarily the subject librarians or liaisons who work with faculty and students in the disciplines. While we found much attention being paid to assessing learning outcomes and the general value of libraries, there is little in the literature that discussed what we consider the most important part of the research process—the liaison librarians who work closely with faculty and students for research and teaching needs and who build relevant collections and provide other tools, resources, and support for these activities.

We also see that the roles that our subject librarians are assuming are changing the nature of their work and that it is clear to us as library administrators that building an effective and productive liaison program is the key to continued engagement and to demonstrating the value of our library to our institution. A recent publication by the Association of Research Libraries discusses how liaison roles are changing in research libraries. According to the authors:

> In the past, libraries focused largely on capturing the end products of scholarship, and the bibliographer model was designed to fulfill that goal. Then, the liaison model evolved, recognizing the need for advanced library research assistance within the disciplines and instruction in general library research processes for students. With increasing pressure on researchers to plan and manage their output, and a growing adoption of open access publishing, research libraries are now compelled to understand and support all processes of instruction and scholarship, which calls for an engagement model. An engaged liaison seeks to enhance scholar productivity,

to empower learners, and to participate in the entire life-cycle of the research, teaching, and learning process.[20]

It is our goal that this book, with contributions from a variety of expert librarians, will provide a framework of tools and techniques for assessing these critical liaison activities. This introductory chapter provides a very general overview of assessment in higher education and in research libraries. The remainder of the book is a series of scholarly articles that examine how academic libraries assess liaison activities and offer recommendations for documenting the impact of programs and services in the various components of a liaison's responsibilities.

Notes

1. Alexander W. Astin and Anthony L. Antonio, *Assessment for Excellence: The Philosophy and Practice of Assessment and Evaluation in Higher Education*, 2nd ed. (Lanham, MD: Rowan and Littlefield, 2012), 3.

2. National Academy of Academic Leadership, "Assessment and Evaluation in Higher Education: Some Concepts and Principles," accessed January 9, 2014, www.thenationalacademy.org/readings/assessandeval.html.

3. Astin and Antonio, *Assessment for Excellence*, 3.

4. National Academy of Academic Leadership, "Assessment and Evaluation."

5. Margaret A. Miller, "The Legitimacy of Assessment," *Chronicle of Higher Education* 53 (September 22, 2006): B24.

6. Richard B. Fletcher et al., "Faculty and Student Conceptions of Assessment in Higher Education," *Higher Education* 64, no. 1 (July 2012): 120.

7. For example, on learner-centered assessment, see Rosario Hernández, "Does Continuous Assessment in Higher Education Support Student Learning?" *Higher Education* 64, no. 4 (October 2012): 489–502, and Karen L. Webber, "The Use of Learner-Centered Assessment in US Colleges and Universities," *Research in Higher Education* 53, no. 2 (March 2012): 201–26; on program assessments, see Megan Rodgers et al., "Improving Academic Program Assessment: A Mixed Methods Study," *Innovative Higher Education* 38, no. 5 (November 2013): 383–95; on issues related to faculty perceptions, see Jordi Trullen and Sebastián Rodríquez, "Faculty Perceptions of Instrumental and Improvement Reasons behind Quality Assessments in Higher Education: The Roles of Participation and Identification," *Studies in Higher Education* 38, no. 5 (2013): 678–92.

8.   Alexander W. Astin et al., "AAHE Assessment Forum: 9 Principles of Good Practice for Assessing Student Learning," American Association for Higher Education, last modified July 25, 1996, www.academicprograms.calpoly.edu/pdfs/assess/nine_principles_good_practice.pdf.

9.   Barrett Havens, "Give Assessment a Fighting Chance," *Chronicle of Higher Education*, November 4, 2013, http://chronicle.com/article/article-content/142773.

10.   LibQUAL+ home page, Association of Research Libraries, accessed January 10, 2014, www.libqual.org/home.

11.   Megan Oakleaf, "Are They Learning? Are We? Learning Outcomes and the Academic Library," *Library Quarterly* 81, no. 1 (January 2011): 61–82, doi:10.1086/657444.

12.   Megan Oakleaf, *Value of Academic Libraries: A Comprehensive Research Review and Report* (Washington, DC: Association of College and Research Libraries, September 2010), www.ala.org/acrl/files/issues/value/val_report.pdf; Library Assessment Conference home page, Association of Research Libraries, accessed January 10, 2014, http://libraryassessment.org.

13.   Martha Kyrillidou and Damon Jaggers, "Current Themes in Academic Library Assessment: Select Papers from the 2010 Library Assessment Conference," *Evidence Based Library and Information Practice* 8, no. 2 (2013): 6.

14.   Jon R. Hufford, "A Review of the Literature on Assessment in Academic and Research Libraries, 2005–2011," *portal: Libraries and the Academy* 13, no. 1 (January 2013): 5–6, doi:10.1353/pla.2013.0005.

15.   For example, on discovery tools and systems, see Kim Durante and Zheng Wang, "Creating an Actionable Assessment Framework for Discovery Services in Academic Libraries," *College and Undergraduate Libraries* 19, no. 2–4 (2012): 215–28, doi:10.1080/10691316.2012.693358; on instructional and information literacy programs, see Brandy Whitlock and Julie Nanavati, "A Systematic Approach to Performative and Authentic Assessment," *Reference Services Review* 41, no. 1 (2013): 32–48; on support of distance education, see Larry Nash White, "Assessment Planning for Distance Education Library Services: Strategic Roadmaps for Determining and Reporting Organizational Performance and Value," *Journal of Library Administration* 50, no. 7–8 (2010): 1017–26, doi:10.1080/01930826.2010.489007; on library spaces and learning commons, see Heather Lea Jackson and Trudi Bellardo Hahn, "Serving Higher Education's Highest Goals: Assessment of the Academic Library as Place," *College and Research Libraries* 72, no. 5 (September 2011): 428–42; and Danuta A. Nitecki, "Space Assessment as a Venue for Defining the Academic Library," *Library Quarterly* 81, no. 1 (January 2011): 27–59, doi:10.1086/657446.

16.   Meredith Gorran Farkas, "Building and Sustaining a Culture of Assessment: Best Practices for Change Leadership," *Reference Services Review* 41, no. 1 (2013): 13–31.

17. Amos Lakos and Shelley E. Phipps, "Creating a Culture of Assessment: A Catalyst for Organizational Change," *portal: Libraries and the Academy* 4, no. 3 (July 2004): 345–61, doi:10.1353/pla.2004.0052.

18. Ibid., 352.

19. Ibid.; Farkas, "Building and Sustaining a Culture of Assessment."

20. Janice M. Jaguszewksi and Karen Williams, *New Roles for New Times: Transforming Liaison Roles in Research Libraries* (Washington, DC: Association of Research Libraries, 2013), 4.

Chapter Two

Programmatic Assessment of Research Services

Informing the Evolution of an Engaged Liaison Librarian Model

Sarah Anne Murphy

Coordinator of Assessment
The Ohio State University Libraries
Columbus, OH

Craig Gibson

Professor and Head of FAES Library
The Ohio State University
Columbus, OH

Academic libraries are developing liaison programs that transcend the traditional collections-focused reference model of liaison service and move toward to a more integrated approach focused on all aspects of knowledge creation, publishing, and research consulting on their campuses. Positioning library liaison programming and liaison librarians in all parts of the research life cycle is now crucial as the complexity of information and the challenge of understanding and optimally using information continue to evolve. This positioning requires expanding the traditional liaison model into the workflows of faculty and students to touch "upstream" and "downstream" phases of the research process and includes activities such as helping graduate students locate potential collaborators or mentors for research projects, assisting faculty with grant projects as part of a research team, identifying demographic data for undergraduates working on a service learning project in a local community, or assisting any of these groups with eventual publication of their findings in a digital repository. Liaison librarians who actively participate in more stages of the research process and the creation of knowledge through the provision of an integrated suite of research services will become more engaged with users. Research services may best be envisioned as an emerging model of research life cycle–focused support—expanding the traditional repertoire of reference skills and research consultations into a more fully engaged participation, at a programmatic level, across the spectrum of research activities on campus.

The challenge for evaluating any emerging model of service is that legacy metrics, usually focused on inputs or output measures, often fail to capture the true impact or value of the service to the academic community. Evaluating a liaison program driven by research services poses special challenges because assessment requires a longitudinal strategic approach. An effective liaison program should develop into an enterprise-level, highly visible initiative that taps the knowledge and expertise of an entire organization. Quality programs grow out of relationship-building activities between subject or liaison librarians and faculty, between library administrators and academic program administrators, and within libraries themselves, across public services, technical services, and information technology units. To achieve integration, liaison librarians must create a flexible programmatic focus for research services that respects the needs of each discipline served. With a programmatic focus, research services can be assessed, while recognizing that different levels of engagement are required from liaison librarians and library organizations as a whole to meet the diverse expectations and needs of faculty, graduate students, and undergraduates.

The Ohio State University Libraries created an "Engaged Librarian Framework" in 2011 to align its liaison services more closely with all other phases of the research life cycle. The framework builds on the strengths of traditional reference and outreach services and consists of five core elements:

- **Research Services:** expert consulting on the full spectrum of scholarly activity, as well as assessment and analysis of user needs
- **Scholarly Communication:** working with constituents on publishing, including open-access publishing and practices associated with deposit of research findings in repositories; assisting faculty and students with understanding copyright and author rights
- **Collection Development:** applying knowledge of scholarly communication trends to local collection development initiatives; effectively managing resources to increase the value of local collections; using collections to increase the value of services supporting faculty research
- **Teaching and Learning:** collaborating with colleagues within the libraries and with teaching faculty to plan, deliver, and improve information literacy instruction within the context of the entire institution
- **Engagement:** deepened, sustained communication, interaction, and partnership with constituents[1]

These five core elements, or "pillars," each have associated compe-tencies and best practices. For example, one of the competencies of the Research Services pillar is "Actively seeking opportunities to foster inter-disciplinary collaborations in the provision of research and information across the campus." An example of a best practice associated with this pillar suggests liaison librarians "regularly [survey] departmental web-sites, listservs, press releases,… and other appropriate sources to identify faculty research interests, announcements of new university initiatives and centers, etc."[2]

While all elements of the framework support research at an institutional level and each subject librarian is responsible for informed knowledge of scholarly communication, collection development, and teaching and learning, research services are envisioned as the undergirding foundation of Ohio State's liaison librarian program. This understanding of research services requires the entire cohort of liaison librarians to support their individual constituents and departments so that library engagement with the research, teaching, and service enterprise results. Because research services support the research life cycle, programmatic assessment of this suite of services is essential to evaluate the success of our relationship-building activities and guide the libraries' development of new services and products that add value. Such assessment requires a multifaceted, longitudinal approach supported by a logic model and detailed evaluation plan.

Development of a Logic Model and Evaluation Plan for Research Services and Library Engagement

A logic model visually represents the sequence of events that lead to a program's intended result. This foundational evaluation tool forces stakeholders to develop and describe programmatic strategy using specific language and terms that facilitate evaluation of the program. In other words, the logic model is a "relatively simple image that reflects how and why your program will work."[3]

The logic model helps an organization to plan and design effective programs and also to systematically implement, evaluate, and communicate the results of its programs. When read from left to right, the logic model pictorially represents a series of *If... then...* statements that connect an organization's investments in a program, or inputs, with its activities, intended audience, and outcomes. Models also consider assumptions and external factors that may shape or influence a program.

There is no right or wrong way to construct a logic model. Not all programmatic outcomes are linear, for example. Instead, stakeholders should focus on creating a logic model that is clear, meaningful, and specific enough to track progress and inform evaluation.[4]

The Ohio State University Libraries use two logic models to guide evaluation of research services and library engagement (figures 2.1 and 2.2). The two models reflect the reality that intended programmatic outcomes for research services and library engagement differ significantly depending on audience. Specifically, the programmatic outcomes and intended impacts the libraries hope to achieve with faculty are not the same as the outcomes and impacts envisioned for undergraduate and graduate students. For example, an intended impact or long-term outcome for research services and library engagement is that faculty will maintain sustained relationships with OSU librarians and services. This intended impact is not included in the undergraduate and graduate students' logic model, because the resources and activities required for the libraries' research services program must be tailored to reach the desired audience and achieve the intended outcomes.

Figure 2.1

Evaluation of Research Services and Library Engagement, Undergraduate and Graduate Students, Logic Model (OSU Libraries)

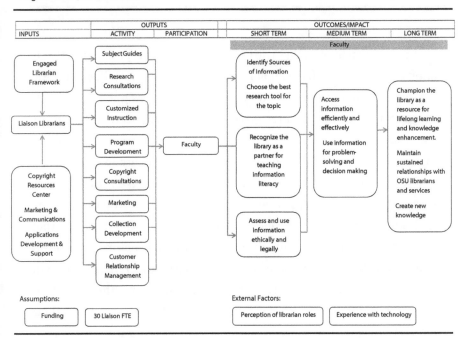

Figure 2.2
Evaluation of Research Services and Library Engagement, Faculty, Logic Model (OSU Libraries)

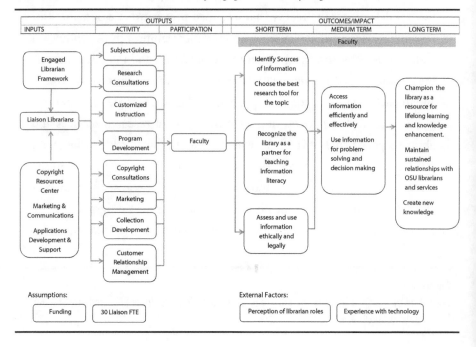

A major benefit of using logic models to ground programmatic evaluation of research services is that logic models offer liaison librarians the flexibility to adapt to the situational needs of their assigned disciplines. The appendix to this chapter provides discipline-specific context for the short-term, medium-term, and long-term outcomes identified in figure 2.1 as applied to business undergraduate and graduate students. For practical purposes, short-term outcomes represent the changes in students' knowledge, attitudes, skills, or aspirations that the libraries hope to witness within one to three years. The libraries hope that participants will achieve medium-term outcomes before graduation and that long-term outcomes of the libraries' research services will be witnessed within one to two years post-graduation. The impact, or intended change, expected of matriculated students as a result of their interaction with the libraries' research services and library engagement program, is grounded in the libraries' aspirational vision and mission, which aim to

- advance student and faculty success
- deliver distinctive content
- foster intellectual connections

The entire statement of the Ohio State University Libraries' vision, mission, and strategic themes is as follows:

Vision

- Advance student and faculty success
- Deliver distinctive content
- Foster intellectual connections

Mission

The Ohio State University Libraries is a dynamic partner and campus leader in advancing discovery and learning for OSU, for the state of Ohio, and for an ever expanding community of world scholars.

We create, acquire, organize, disseminate, and preserve scholarship in traditional and digital forms; we foster an environment conducive to academic inquiry, scholarly communication, creative achievement, and lifelong learning; we help students become information literate and globally aware; and we contribute to the University's drive to eminence in teaching, research and service.

Strategic Themes

Services: Develop and refine user-centered services which integrate libraries and library faculty and staff into environments where users work and interact.

Collections: Manage the evolution of the Libraries' information resources to match the needs and behaviors of users, and to reflect the changing technologies and practices in publishing, research and teaching.

Library as Intellectual Crossroads: Enhance the Libraries' place as a cultural, social, and intellectual crossroads—a physical and virtual place for cultivating intellectual inquiry and the development of critical thinking skills, promoting academic discourse, and fostering lifelong learning and knowledge enhancement.

Innovative Leadership: Establish the Libraries as a national leader in the integration of intellectual content and services within the larger world of ideas and knowledge.

Infrastructure: Foster a supportive, respectful and diverse work environment that utilizes and develops the best talents of the Libraries' faculty and staff. Establish an organizational culture which embraces innovation and change, promotes continued improvement, and judiciously allocates its resources to support the University's strategic needs.[5]

Thus, if reading the logic model provided in figure 2.1 from left to right, the reader may infer that

IF

The business liaison librarian, with the support of the Engaged Librarian Framework and the libraries' Copyright Resources Center, Marketing and Communications department, and Applications Development and Support department, creates subject guides and provides research consultations, customized instruction, and collections development services for undergraduate and graduate students

THEN

Within one to three years, undergraduate and graduate students will be able to

1. define an information need;
2. identify sources of information; and
3. choose the best research tool for the topic.

THEN

By graduation, undergraduate and graduate students will be able to

1. access information efficiently and effectively.

THEN

Within one to two years post-matriculation, undergraduate and graduate students will be able to

1. use information for problem solving and decision making;
2. create new knowledge; and
3. recognize the library as a resource for lifelong learning and knowledge enhancement.

The Evaluation Plan

A logic model provides focus for an evaluation plan so that the evaluators can direct resources to determine whether the program was of value to stakeholders. The logic model guides the formulation of formative and summative evaluation questions from three programmatic perspectives: context, implementation, and results. While context questions "explore issues of program relationships and capacity," implementation questions focus on quantity and quality, or "the extent to which activities were executed as planned."[6] Both context and implementation questions drive formative evaluation, which helps stakeholders to improve a program. Such questions are periodically asked throughout a program. Results questions drive summative evaluation, focusing on outputs, outcomes, and impact to demonstrate the results of a program for participants, stakeholders, and the broader community. Results questions are typically asked on completion of a program or following implementation of a specific programmatic phase.

Table 2.1 presents an evaluation plan written for the OSU Libraries' research services and library engagement program. Note that not every aspect of the libraries' research services and library engagement program for faculty and undergraduate and graduate students is measured. The plan is focused on gathering information that may best inform the development of the program or articulate its results. It also considers the audience for each question and their use of the evaluation. For example, it may help undergraduates to know that individuals who use the libraries' research consultation services when writing papers longer than five pages experience less frustration and achieve better results. Liaison librarians also need to know whether their efforts to enhance campus information literacy instruction result in more sustained relationships with teaching faculty.

Questions are linked to indicators, which represent evidence of progress towards an intended goal. While indicators should be SMART—Specific, Measureable, Action-oriented, Realistic, and Timed—it is important to note that not all indicators are quantitative in nature. To determine whether faculty recognize the library as a partner for teaching information literacy, for example, a qualitative indicator may be more appropriate. Surveys or focus groups structured to query faculty on their experience integrating information literacy concepts into their courses may reveal valuable insights. Proof that liaison librarians' efforts to enhance campus information literacy instruction and thus maintain sustained relationships with faculty may be obtained from both qualitative and quantitative sources.

Table 2.1
Evaluation of Research Services and Library Engagement, Evaluation Plan (OSU Libraries)

Evaluation Focus Area	Audience	Question	Use	Indicators
Relationships	Liaison Librarians	Are faculty working with liaison librarians to plan and deliver information literacy instruction?	Program improvement & planning/ Program promotion	Teaching collaborations with faculty increase 15% by 2016
		Are liaison librarians effectively marketing library services for enhancing information literacy instruction to faculty?	Program improvement & planning/ Program promotion	Teaching collaborations with faculty increase 15% by 2016
Quantity & Quality	Undergraduates	How many undergraduate students consult a librarian for help to write a paper or report greater than 5 pages?	Program improvement & planning/ Program promotion	Number of undergraduate students who use the Libraries research consultation services to help write a paper or report greater than 5 pages
	Graduates	How many graduate students use the Libraries' Research Consultation Services more than 2 times a year?	Evaluation	Number of graduate students who use the Libraries' Research Consultation Services more than 2 times in one year.
	Faculty	How many faculty use the Libraries' Research Consultation Services more than 2 times a year?	Evaluation	Number of faculty who use the Libraries' Research Consultation Services more than 2 times in one year.
		How often do faculty request liaison librarian services to enhance information literacy instruction for the same course in subsequent years?	Evaluation/ Program improvement & planning/ Program promotion	Number of repeat information literacy instruction customers

Table 2.1 ...(Continued)
Evaluation of Research Services and Library Engagement, Evaluation Plan (OSU Libraries)

Evaluation Focus Area	Audience	Question	Use	Indicators
Outcomes	Undergraduates	Can undergraduate students access information efficiently and effectively?	Evaluation	3rd year students access information efficiently and effectively
		Do undergraduate students formulate considered and reasoned ethical judgments when assessing and using information?	University accreditation/ Evaluation	3rd year students assess and use information ethically and legally
	Graduates	Do graduate students access information efficiently and effectively to create new knowledge?	Cost benefit analysis/ Program improvement & planning	Graduate students access information efficiently and effectively to create new knowledge
	Faculty	Do faculty negotiate with liaison librarians on timing, purpose, and learning outcomes for information literacy instruction?	Program improvement & planning/ Evaluation	Faculty recognize the library as a partner for teaching information literacy
		Do faculty access information efficiently and effectively to create new knowledge?	Cost benefit analysis/ Program improvement & planning	Faculty access information efficiently and effectively to create new knowledge
	Office of Academic Affairs	Do undergraduate students formulate considered and reasoned ethical judgments when assessing and using information?	University accreditation	3rd year students assess and use information ethically and legally

Indicators are last linked to a data-gathering plan, which identifies either existing resources for gathering quantitative or qualitative information or activities such as surveys that are needed to collect information to be analyzed. Table 2.2 outlines the data-gathering plan for the OSU Libraries' research services and library engagement program. Existing data sources include the libraries' LibAnswers and TEACH databases, both flexible data-collection tools that allow the libraries to collect information on a number of library services. Using LibAnswers, librar-

Table 2.2
Evaluation of Research Services and Library Engagement, Data Gathering Plan (OSU Libraries)

Focus Area	Indicators	Data Gathering Plan
Relationships	Teaching collaborations with faculty increase 15% by 2016	TEACH Database
Quantity & Quality	Number of undergraduate students who use the Libraries Research Consultation Services to help write a paper or report greater than 5 pages	LibAnswers; NSSE (to determine the % of 1st and 3rd year undergraduate students who report writing a paper of 5 pages or more who used the Libraries' research consultation services)
	Number of graduate students who use the Libraries' Research Consultation Services more than 2 times in one year	LibAnswers
	Number of faculty who use the Libraries' Research Consultation Services more than 2 times in one year	LibAnswers
	Number of repeat information literacy instruction customers	TEACH Database
Outcomes	3rd year students assess information efficiently and effectively	Cohort study
	Graduate students access information efficiently and effectively to create new knowledge	LibQUAL Usage Data
	Faculty recognize the library as a partner for teaching information literacy	TEACH Database Faculty Survey/Focus Groups
	Faculty access information efficiently and effectively to create new knowledge	LibQUAL Usage Data Academic Analytics?

ians may record information regarding research consultations, including patron demographics, question format, and the time spent answering the question. Data regarding question format, patron discipline, and the time required to answer the question are important for informing assignment of liaison librarian time and responsibilities. The libraries' TEACH database operates on the LibAnalytics platform and currently serves as means to centrally collect ARL Instruction statistics and record learning outcomes for individual library instruction activities.

Other existing sources of information to inform evaluation of the libraries' liaison program include the open comments students and faculty provide via the libraries semiannual administration of LibQUAL. In past surveys, both user populations have provided rich comments on their interactions with liaison librarians. The National Survey of Student Engagement (NSSE) provides context by highlighting how often undergraduate students are assigned research papers or reports longer than five pages. The university's Institutional Research and Planning department administers this survey triannually to all first-year students and seniors. Recent results show that while 64 percent of all first-year respondents wrote a paper or a report at least one to four times during the school year in 2007, 50 percent of seniors wrote a twenty-plus-page report or paper more than five times during the school year. In 2010, while 57 percent of all first-year respondents wrote a paper or report at least one to four times during the school year, 54 percent of seniors wrote a twenty-plus-page paper or report more than five times during the school year. Not surprisingly, seniors taking the 2007 and 2010 surveys were more likely to write a paper or report longer than twenty pages than first-year students.

To further understand the impact of the research services and library engagement program on faculty, focus groups and cohort studies will need to be designed and executed to supplement the information gathered from existing sources. The data-gathering plan highlights this need and prompts individuals responsible for executing the program evaluation plan to contract with an independent evaluator or develop these assessments internally. Ideally, data-gathering efforts will be structured to collect information for each indicator at set points in time, such as before the implementation of a major program phase and on completion of a program for comparison purposes.

Conclusion

Evaluating a library liaison program focused on research services requires an assessment model that measures impact across time (multiple years), leverages multiple data sources, and allows for customization and flexibility as liaison librarians interact with faculty and students in a variety of disciplines. The research services program at the Ohio State University Libraries serves as the foundation of the libraries' Engaged Librarian Framework, weaving research support with scholarly communication, collection development, teaching and learning, and engagement itself. To advance the libraries' research services program, the coordinated efforts of individuals across the libraries' organization are required. These efforts are supported by the definitions and best practices identified in the framework, the logic model, and the corresponding evaluation plan. This documentation will guide the libraries toward realizing its long-term goals—sustained interaction with faculty and students, collaboration and reciprocity between the libraries and their constituents, enhanced teaching and learning practices, and creation of new knowledge and scholarship.

Research services, as an integrated suite of research support rooted in liaison librarianship, must include the expertise of scholarly communication, copyright, and collection development staff, as well as data and information literacy specialists, to achieve the greatest impact. Focused assessment of the research services program will better position the libraries to demonstrate sustained value in supporting the scholarly, teaching and learning, and service missions of the university.

Notes

1. Ohio State University Libraries, "A Framework for the Engaged Librarian: Building on Our Strengths," last modified October 22, 2012, https://carmenwiki.osu. edu/download/attachments/37010332/Engaged+Librarian+Document.pdf?version=1 &modificationDate=1362663472574.

2. Ibid., 2.

3. W. K. Kellogg Foundation, *Logic Model Development Guide* (Battle Creek, MI: W. K. Kellogg Foundation, 1998, updated January 2004), 7, www.wkkf.org/knowledge-center/resources/2006/02/wk-kellogg-foundation-logic-model-development-guide.aspx.

4. University of Wisconsin Extension, *Enhancing Program Performance with Logic Models* (University of Wisconsin-Extension, February 2003), 17, www.uwex.edu/ces/pdande/evaluation/pdf/lmcourseall.pdf.

5. Ohio State University Libraries, "Vision, Mission, Strategic Themes," accessed June 18, 2014, http://library.osu.edu/about/administration/vision-mission-strategic-themes.

6. W. K. Kellogg Foundation, *Logic Model Development Guide*, 36–37.

Appendix 2.1: Situation Statement (Business)

Rapid growth and changes in the information landscape challenge students to use information both efficiently and effectively in order to bring clarity, solve problems, and create new knowledge. The Fisher College of Business prepares students to make positive contributions to their communities and the world at large as future business leaders, entrepreneurs, and academics. The OSU Libraries supports college initiatives by fostering an environment conducive to academic inquiry, scholarly communication, creative achievement, and lifelong learning.

As information behavior impacts business success, an appreciation for lifelong learning, along with the skills to identify, locate, evaluate, and effectively use information, is especially important for business leaders.[1]

Both public and academic libraries support small to medium-sized businesses' information needs. In 2010 alone, US public libraries provided services to business owners and employees 2.8 million times every month.[2] As small businesses make up 99.7 percent of US employers and generate 46 percent of the country's private-sector output, libraries support job creation and economic growth.[3]

Notes

1.   Liwen Qiw Vaughan, "The Contribution of Information to Business Success: A LISREL Model Analysis of Manufacturers in Shanghai," *Information Processing and Management* 35, no. 2 (March 1999): 193–208.

2.   OCLC, *How Libraries Stack Up: 2010* (Dublin, OH: OCLC, 2010), www.oclc.org/content/dam/oclc/reports/pdfs/214109usf_how_libraries_stack_up.pdf.

3.   US Small Business Administration, *Frequently Asked Questions*, September 2012, 1, www.sba.gov/sites/default/files/FAQ_Sept_2012.pdf.

Chapter Three

Assessment of Teaching, Learning, and Literacies

Ellysa Stern Cahoy
Education Librarian and Assistant Director
The Pennsylvania Center for the Book
The Pennsylvania State University Libraries
University Park, PA

Course-related, credit-based, and informal instruction occupies a significant portion of a liaison librarian's responsibilities. Whether teaching formal, in-person library research classes, providing individualized reference consultations, or developing online learning objects, creative, responsive pedagogy with demonstrable learning impact is central to effective liaison librarianship.

This chapter will focus on assessment of a liaison librarian's instructional programs and initiatives. It will identify and describe assessment strategies that provide academic libraries with a unified portrait of the scope and impact of liaison librarians' teaching initiatives. While individually conducted assessment practices, such as peer review of course-related instruction, are important, assessing a unified program of instruction can provide a more comprehensive depiction of a liaison librarian's greatest areas of instructional impact and will identify audiences or initiatives needing more attention or improvement. A systematic approach to assessing liaison instruction will also provide a more unified view of the impact of library instruction on student learning and will add strength to the imperative to embed information literacy learning outcomes within the curriculum.

Specific tactics that will be described and outlined include:

- identifying and creating a curriculum map of academic department or college courses to scaffold information literacy instruction and identify learning gaps
- tailoring an assessment program to provide multiple perspectives (student, instructor, and peer assessment) on liaison librarians' instructional effectiveness.
- implementing strategies for developing institutional information literacy learning outcomes.
- designing professional development programs that increase and build upon liaisons' pedagogical approaches.

Undoubtedly, the teaching role of the liaison librarian is central to student acquisition of critical-thinking and information literacy skills; these strategies will help the academic library define, build, and highlight these instructional successes for enhanced embeddedness and instructional collaboration across the curriculum.

Defining Information Literacy and Learning Goals

In her presentation on assessment at the Association of College and Research Libraries/Institute for Information Literacy Immersion program, Debra Gilchrist outlined a foundation for information literacy assessment, shown in figure 3.1.

At the base of the structure is the campus philosophy (or definition) of information literacy. On some campuses, this may be framed instead as critical thinking. Regardless of the terminology used, this statement underscores how information skills are framed locally within the institution. Here is an example of an information literacy definition statement from the University of Texas at Dallas:

Figure 3.1
Information Literacy Learning Foundation for Assessment (Source: Debra Gilchrist, "Improving Student Learning: Outcomes Assessment and Information Literacy Instruction" [paper presented at the ACRL/IIL Immersion, University of Colorado, Colorado Springs, 2002]).

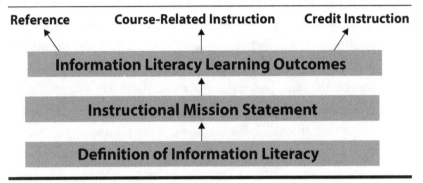

Information Literacy is defined as the ability to locate, evaluate, manage, and use information from a variety of sources, both print and electronic, for problem solving, decision-making, and research.[1]

Moving up from the articulated philosophy is the campus mission with regard to information literacy. In a sentence (or two), how will our students benefit from effective information literacy instruction? An example of a campus information literacy mission statement is the following, also from the UT Dallas Libraries:

Information Literacy at the University of Texas at Dallas is a means for students, faculty, staff and community users to develop library research skills, information literacy ability and competent information use as a part of lifelong learning.[2]

This vision-centered statement should underscore the local focus on information literacy relative to the campus's student population and specific needs. From the mission statement, measurable learning outcomes are articulated that identify what students are expected to learn from information literacy instruction. Good learning outcomes translate intentions into actions, describe what students should demonstrate or produce, and always use action verbs. Further, effective learning outcomes map to practices, are collaboratively authored, reflect or complement existing national criteria, and perhaps most significantly, are readily measurable through assessment.[3] Learning outcomes should also map with significant documents at the state, regional, and national level. For example, many current instances of academic information literacy learning outcomes align closely with the ACRL *Information Literacy Competency Standards for Higher Education*.[4] Ideally, the learning outcomes should not exist in isolation (i.e., on a library's Learning Services web page) but should be fully created in tandem with institution-wide undergraduate- or graduate-level student learning outcomes. As an example, the University of Minnesota Undergraduate Student Learning Outcomes are broad and integrate information use and evaluation:

> At the time of receiving a bachelor's degree, students:
> - Can identify, define, and solve problems
> - Can locate and critically evaluate information
> - Have mastered a body of knowledge and a mode of inquiry
> - Understand diverse philosophies and cultures within and across societies
> - Can communicate effectively
> - Understand the role of creativity, innovation, discovery, and expression across disciplines
> - Have acquired skills for effective citizenship and lifelong learning[5]

These outcomes provide an entry point for information literacy instruction within the curriculum, whether the course instructor or the librarian provides the instruction. The outcomes also signify the main areas in which student learning will be structured, and therefore assessed, at the university-wide level. The University of Minnesota example provides entry points for information literacy (or critical-thinking) instruction in all of the articulated outcomes, particularly Outcome 2 ("Can locate and critically evaluate information"). Once institution-wide learning outcomes are in place, the work of mapping curriculum and creating college-, department-, and course-level learning outcomes can begin.

Curriculum Mapping

A liaison librarian can easily see where to embed library instruction once the scope and sequence of an institution's curriculum is fully mapped and readily understood. Jacobs identifies curriculum mapping as "a procedure that promotes the creation of a visual representation of curriculum based on real time information."[6] Curriculum mapping occurs in six discrete steps: (1) Individual course instructors map their learning goals and outcomes. (2) All of the instructors of a specific course bring together and aggregate their individual course maps. (3) Courses are aggregately mapped in a specific program, major, or sequence of courses. (4) Areas of strength, weakness, and unaddressed need are identified. (5) Individual courses are revised according to the mapping findings and perceived areas of needed revision or attention. (6) Newly revised, the curriculum is revisited regularly to see if the mapping needs to be changed, enriched, or updated.[7]

For liaison librarians, curriculum mapping presents a ripe opportunity for collaboration. This is a chance to work closely with academic departments, to understand deeply their individual courses, majors and programs of study, and their overall curriculum. Perhaps most significant, curriculum mapping allows teaching faculty and librarians to look expansively across a major, program of study, and entire college or university to see where students begin the process of finding, using, and creating information and how those skills progress and are enriched throughout the academic curriculum. Curriculum mapping should expose opportunities to embed the acquisition of research, technology, and content-creation skills at every level of student learning. This does not mean that librarians have to teach these information skills at every stage of learning and in every class. More important is mapping and designing information-use–focused learning outcomes appropriate to levels of learning and creating enrichment tools (guides, tutorials, curriculum materials) to be used in support of student acquisition of these central skills and digital literacies. Moser et al. note, "The program must be couched in terms that are relevant to all campus stakeholders, not just to librarians. The overarching mission of a curriculum mapping project should be to achieve an understanding of shared goals, clarify how those goals fit within an educational program, and generate collaborative ideas for how to accomplish those goals."[8]

The Ithaka S+R US Faculty Survey 2012 presents food for thought on the role of academic librarians in teaching students information literacy learning outcomes. In the survey, participating faculty were asked about the role of the library in their work and specifically the role of the library and librarians as "Undergraduate Information Literacy Teacher," articulated as "The library helps undergraduates develop research, critical analysis, and information literacy skills."[9] Responding faculty saw the library's most important role as buyer (80 percent), and less than 60 percent of faculty saw the role of librarians as undergraduate information literacy teacher.[10] This response differed further by discipline, with humanists most frequently (approximately 70 percent) seeing the role of the librarian as information literacy instructor, versus social sciences faculty (just under 60 percent) and sciences faculty (just over 40 percent).[11]

Similarly, Arendt and Lott's article, "What Liaisons Say about Themselves and What Faculty Say about Their Liaisons: A US Survey," investigates the services liaison librarians provide and the importance that faculty place upon those services. In this study, faculty felt that library instruction and integration of library-related skills into the curriculum were less important than librarians' perceptions of the same issues. The authors note, "Liaisons may face a challenge in finding faculty who believe in the importance of information literacy enough to take the time to incorporate the library into the classroom."[12]

Both of these studies identify a future course for librarians and information literacy instruction, reinforcing the significance of curriculum mapping as a liaison outreach strategy. Faculty may see libraries and librarians primarily as gateway to information, buyer, and repository.[13] While this does not mean that a librarian's instructional work is unappreciated, it does reinforce the need to work collaboratively with faculty to embed information literacy (and digital literacies in general) within the curriculum. The job of teaching information use and knowledge-creation skills is not one solely covered by liaison librarians, and curriculum mapping ensures that the acquisition of these central abilities occurs across the curriculum, regardless of whether librarian or course instructor is imparting the knowledge and experiential learning to students.

Oakleaf presents an idea that goes beyond curriculum mapping: a library mission impact map. This tool lays out all campus goals and learning outcomes in one column, while listing existing library services, tutorials and resources, and library departments across the top of the map. Identifying areas of overlap with regard to the library and campus goals and learning outcomes, it shows which areas of importance are well-covered and where new services or methods of outreach may need to be developed to support students. Oakleaf points out that once the areas are mapped, the next task is to assess the impact.[14] Figure 3.2 is an example mission impact map from Oakleaf's article, illustrating how the impact map visualizes the contribution of library services towards student support and success.

Types of Assessment

Once learning outcomes have been agreed upon and articulated, it is time to assess the impact and effectiveness of the instruction. Murtha, Stec, and Wilt identify five steps in a systematic approach to information literacy assessment: (1) Determine the purpose of the assessment. (2)

Figure 3.2

Mission Impact Map (Source: Megan Oakleaf, "Are They Learning? Are We? Learning Outcomes and the Academic Library," *Library Quarterly* 81, no. 1 [January 2011]: 69, doi:10.1086/657444.)

Campus Needs, Goals, and Outcomes	Reference Services	Instructional Services	Circulation	Reserves	Interlibrary Loan	Acquisitions	Collections	Special Collections and Archives	Physical Space
Student enrollment		X						X	X
Student retention	X	X	X	X			X		
Student graduation rates	X	X	X	X			X		
Student success	X	X							X
Student achievement	X	X							
Student learning	X	X							
Student experience									X
Faculty research output		X			X	X	X	X	
Faculty grant funding		X			X	X	X	X	
Faculty teaching		X		X					

Define and describe what "good teaching" means in the context of the program. (This could go back to the campus or institution's information literacy definition or mission statement.) (3) Select the methodologies to be used. (4) Develop or select tools with which to apply the methodologies. (5) Develop standard processes and procedures for implementing and interpreting the assessment.[15]

For liaison librarians, information literacy assessment may come into play at several different levels, from the individual to the institution: formative assessment of library instruction, summative assessment of library instruction, library-wide assessment of student learning and library instruction, and institution-wide assessment of student learning. Like the curriculum map, each level of assessment (from individual to institutional) informs the next and shows the broad impact of information literacy learning outcomes and embedded instruction.

Formative assessment exists primarily for the benefit of an individual librarian. It is a more informal assessment that helps the library instructor understand the strengths and weaknesses of his or her instructional approaches. Formative assessment can be conducted for course-related instruction sessions or for credit-bearing instruction conducted online or in person. The goal of formative assessment is simply to provide feedback and to encourage a dialogue on teaching effectiveness and improvement.

Formative assessment of library instruction can include informal observation of instruction, teaching portfolios, peer review, personal reflections, citation analysis, and student or faculty questionnaires.[16] Formative assessment should be done in tandem with professional development to improve instruction in highlighted areas of need.

Summative assessment is conducted in a more formal and documented manner than formative evaluation. It is typically administered during a set time period adjacent to an annual review or a tenure review and may focus more on formal methods of assessment, such as student and instructor evaluations, peer review of instruction, or focused citation analysis of student works. Any assessment, either formative or summative, should be guided by the institution's information literacy mission and should use the learning outcomes articulated at the appropriate level (university, college, department, course) to measure the impact of instruction.

With both formative and summative assessment, there is the question of when to assess. For many librarians providing course-related instruction, the immediate inclination may be to assess immediately after an instruction session. At the end of class, librarians may point students toward a short survey asking about instructional gains and areas of need. Similarly, librarians may contact teaching faculty shortly after class to gain feedback (either through a formal survey or through a more informal reflection) from the instructor on the impact of the librarian's work with the class. While this assessment will provide a snapshot of the impact of the instruction immediately after delivery to students, waiting until the end of the semester or course period to assess students and instructors may be more beneficial. This allows the students to utilize their new knowledge, complete relevant projects, and receive a project or course grade that should reflect the degree to which they internalized and put to use new information literacy skills. End-of-term assessment is focused more on the acquisition of skills and the impact of instruction than on the affect and instructional effect of the librarian. Example questions asked within end-of-term assessment could include: "Is this a true statement? The library instruction that I received this semester helped me better understand how to find and use library resources." "If you used library resources, do you feel that they helped you to achieve a higher grade on your assignments?" These questions are easy to answer since each requires only a yes or no response and allows for the long-term impact of the instruction to be assessed. Surveying students and instructors at the end of the semester brings a risk that there may be a lower response rate, but with a focused methodology (such as sending paper surveys to instructors to have students fill out during class time), responses should not be lost.

Both formative and summative peer review of instruction should be conducted. This is an important opportunity for dialogue with an experienced colleague and fellow instructor about instructional improvement. It is best to select a peer reviewer who has a wealth of instructional experience, has proven success in the classroom, and is familiar with the level or type of instruction under review. For example, subject librarians may wish to have a fellow librarian in a closely related subject area peer-review their instructional session. The peer reviewer can also write a letter summarizing his or her assessment of the librarian's instructional effectiveness for use in an annual or tenure review.

To be analyzed at the library-wide level, summative assessment of instruction (via students, teaching faculty, and peer evaluation) should be required at set intervals for liaison librarians with teaching responsibilities. An example of a policy requiring assessment of course-related instruction at Penn State University is available online.[17] If assessment of course-related (and credit) instruction is required, all efforts should be made to have the assessment data collected in a centralized portal, where the data can be easily exported out and analyzed at a variety of levels across the library. This aggregated data should be analyzed regularly for instructional trends. The findings should be shared widely within the library, as well as across campus, as a vehicle for promoting liaison librarians' teaching contributions and overall effectiveness.

At the library-wide level, instructional assessment can complement and add depth to more straightforward findings, such as the number of instructional sessions taught by librarians in a semester. While it is impressive to hear that hundreds of classes were taught by liaison librarians in a twelve-month period, it is more significant to note data from instructional assessment, such as "95 percent of all students receiving library instruction in 2013 felt that they were better able to find and use library materials as a result of the instruction" or "90 percent of all students receiving library instruction felt that they received a higher grade in their course as a result of their ability to better find, evaluate, and use information."

If possible, it is also important to apply instructional assessment to more informal teaching initiatives, such as orientation events, tours, outreach to specialized groups, and special programs. This assessment data can complement more formal instructional assessment data and provide a more complete portrait of the range, scope, and pedagogical reach of liaison librarians' instructional impact.

In *Value of Academic Libraries: A Comprehensive Research Review and Report*, Oakleaf explains the breadth of research on assessment of student learning outcomes and discusses the challenges in demonstrating the library's overall impact in student learning and acquisition of information literacy and critical-thinking skills.[18] While it is important to communicate the impact of instruction broadly, it becomes more difficult to tacitly describe the library's impact on student retention, graduation, and job placement success with regard to instructional initiatives. Oakleaf's report provides a graphic (figure 3.3) that explains the areas in which academic libraries can consider showing impact with regard to learning, success, or enrollment.

Oakleaf notes, "Academic librarians require systematic, coherent, and connected evidence to establish the role of libraries in student learning. Assessment management systems provide the structure that is absolutely critical to establishing a clear picture of how academic libraries contribute to student learning."[19] Without an assessment management system, it

Figure 3.3

Surrogates for Student Learning (Source: Megan Oakleaf, *Value of Academic Libraries: A Comprehensive Research Review and Report* [Washington, DC: Association of College and Research Libraries, September 2010], 41, http://www.ala.org/acrl/files/issues/value/val_report.pdf).

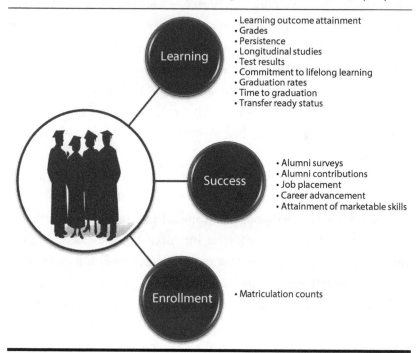

will be more difficult to draw together disparate data groups to represent the library's impact on academic success as a whole. *Value of Academic Libraries* lists many different assessment management systems, including eLumen, TrackDat, and Blackboard's Learn Assessment Module.[20]

Value of Academic Libraries also notes opportunities for participating more broadly in national higher education assessments. These can include the American Association of Colleges and Universities (AAC&U) VALUE project or more campus-based student assessments, such as the Measure of Academic Proficiency (MAP), the College Assessment of Academic Proficiency (CAAP), or the Collegiate Learning Assessment (CAP).[21] The AAC&U VALUE project is focused on assessing student achievement with regard to the LEAP Essential Learning Outcomes.

These learning outcomes are designed to prepare students for current and future intellectual challenges in the areas of content knowledge, critical thinking (including information literacy), personal and social responsibility, and integrative and applied learning. The project has created rubrics around these outcomes that encourage colleges and universities to conduct assessment of authentic student work in a manner that is readily correlated with other peer institutions.[22]

Professional Development

Learning how to reach and teach students effectively is a continuous process, and professional development goes hand-in-hand with regular assessment of liaison instructional activities. Walter points out that "instructional improvement" activities take different forms, including developmental workshops; programs designed to provide feedback on teaching, such as peer review of instruction; instructional grants and other incentives to improve instruction; and opportunities to discuss instructional issues on a broader level with colleagues throughout the library and university.[23] Central among these issues is teaching librarians why we assess and how to assess. Oakleaf identifies several areas of significance for assessment-related professional development: developing an assessment plan, conceptualizing the library impact on learning, defining an action plan for personalized assessment, identifying assessment tools, and communicating library impact.[24] New liaison librarians at an institution should receive an overview of assessment practices and become well acquainted with any policies recommending or mandating regular instructional assessment. This orientation should include hands-on work with any data management software used for assessment, as well as an overview of any resources, including data analysis staff, and technology, such as clickers or other hardware or software, that can be used to conduct instructional assessment. In addition to this orientation, regular, library-wide discussions should be held to address how to create an assessment plan, design instructional instruments, and navigate processes for aggregating instructional assessment data to demonstrate impact. It is also important to talk with liaison librarians about how to best show evidence of instructional impact and teaching innovation within their individual dossiers or annual review documents through the use of assessment data analysis, teaching port-folios, or other means. Assessment should always be a central topic for professional development and is one that can bring together all levels of liaison librarians to collaboratively demonstrate impact and share best assessment practices.

Establishing a formal community of practice helps build a structure around regular instructional professional development for liaison librar-ians. The University of Michigan's Instructor College serves as a model for this type of professional development, in which a sequential curriculum was implemented in five different areas: assessment, learning theory and instructional design, presentation skills, technology, and working with content. Additionally, new instruction librarians receive founda-tion sessions in areas that include an overall orientation to instruction, marketing, working with faculty, and planning an instruction session.[25] This formalized professional development coalesces a community around instructional practices and enables a continued conversation between new and veteran teaching librarians.

Creating a Culture of Assessment

Designing effective information literacy assessment involves thoughtful consideration of the following questions: What do you want the student to be able to do? What does the student need to know in order to accom-plish this? What is the best way to provide content or teach in order to facilitate learning? How will the student demonstrate the learning? And finally, how will you assess the student's ability?[26] Iannuzzi asserts, "There are at least four levels at which we should assess information literacy outcomes: within the library; in the classroom; on campus; and beyond the campus."[27] While assessment within the library and in the classroom may have merged due to the advent of online resources in the past few decades, Iannuzzi's statement underscores the importance of scaffolding assessment efforts in such a way that they readily incorporate findings at both narrower and broader levels of instruction. Creating a culture of assessment that is mobilized to analyze the impact of information literacy instruction at multiple levels within the institution requires sustained collaborative partnerships outside the library, with teaching faculty across the university, and university administrators.

Oakleaf, Millet, and Kraus present a structure for uniting community around information literacy assessment. The authors, using Trinity University as their model, share how they brought together the campus community to create information literacy rubrics that were adopted for institution-wide information literacy assessment.[28] At Trinity, a campus information literacy assessment climate was created using the following strategies: (1) Author a shared and local information literacy definition; (2) Create and conduct a series of information literacy–focused workshops and grants; (3) Create and utilize rubrics for information literacy assessment. The rubrics were collaboratively created systems for grading and assessing student acquisition of specific information literacy learning outcomes. This is just one example of the variety of information literacy assessment–focused case studies that exist in the literature. Finding the right approach for your institution's instructional goals is essential. Assessment can take many forms; in its best incarnation, it tells the lasting story of how liaison librarians partner with teaching faculty to equip students with critical-thinking skills essential for academic success.

Notes

1. Eugene McDermott Library, "Information Literacy Policy and Goals," University of Texas at Dallas, accessed 10/31/2013. www.utdallas.edu/library/about/policies/infolitpolicy.html.

2. Ibid.

3. Peggy L. Maki, *Assessing for Learning: Building a Sustainable Commitment across the Institution* (Sterling, VA: Stylus Publishing, 2010).

4. Association of College and Research Libraries, *Information Literacy Competency Standards for Higher Education* (Chicago: American Library Association, 2000), www.ala.org/acrl/files/standards/standards.pdf.

5. University of Minnesota, "Student Learning and Development," last modified July 30, 2013, www.slo.umn.edu/index.html.

6. Kay Pippin Uchiyama and Jean L. Radin, "Curriculum Mapping in Higher Education: A Vehicle for Collaboration," *Innovative Higher Education* 33, no. 4 (June 24, 2008): 272.

7. Ibid.

8. Mary Moser et al., "A More Perfect Union: Campus Collaborations for Curriculum Mapping Information Literacy Outcomes," in *A Declaration of Interdependence: Proceedings of the ACRL 2011 Conference, March 30–April 2, 2011, Philadelphia, Pa.* (Chicago: Association of College and Research Libraries, 2011): 334, www.ala.org/acrl/files/conferences/confsandpreconfs/national/2011/papers/more_perfect_union.pdf.

9. Deanna Marcum and Roger C. Schonfeld, "Ithaka S+R US Faculty Survey 2012" (presentation, Spring CNI Membership Meeting, San Antonio, TX, April 5, 2013), 27, www.sr.ithaka.org/sites/default/files/reports/Ithaka_SR_US_Faculty_Survey_2012_presentation_4_5_2013.pdf.

10. Ibid., 28.

11. Ibid., 30.

12. Julie Arendt and Megan Lotts, "What Liaisons Say about Themselves and What Faculty Say about Their Liaisons: A US Survey," *portal: Libraries and the Academy* 12, no. 2 (2012): 173, doi:10.1353/pla.2012.0015.

13. Marcum and Schonfeld and Housewright, "Ithaka S+R US Faculty Survey," 28.

14. Megan Oakleaf, "Are They Learning? Are We? Learning Outcomes and the Academic Library," *Library Quarterly* 81, no. 1 (January 2011): 61–82, doi:10.1086/657444.

15. Leslie Murtha, Eileen Stec, and Marilyn Wilt, "Using Assessment as a Tool to Improve Learning: An IFLA Workshop," *IFLA Journal* 32, no. 4 (2006): 294–309.

16. Ibid., 297.

17. Penn State University Libraries, "Guideline UL-ING03 Assessment of Course Related Instruction," last revised August 2007, https://www.libraries.psu.edu/psul/policies/uling03.html.

18. Megan Oakleaf, *Value of Academic Libraries: A Comprehensive Research Review and Report* (Washington, DC: Association of College and Research Libraries, September 2010), http://www.ala.org/acrl/files/issues/value/val_report.pdf.

19. Ibid., 117.

20. Ibid., 45.

21. Ibid., 43–44.

22. Association of American Colleges and Universities, "VALUE: Valid Assessment of Learning in Undergraduate Education," accessed 10/31/2014. www.aacu.org/value/index.cfm.

23. Scott Walter, "Librarians as Teachers: A Qualitative Inquiry into Professional Identity," *College and Research Libraries* 69, no. 1 (January 2008): 51–71.

24. Oakleaf, Megan. 2011. "Are They Learning ? Are We ? Learning Outcomes and the Academic Library." Library Quarterly 81: 61–82. (citation on pg. 74–75).

25. Patricia Yocum et al., "Instructor College: Staff Development for Library Instructors" (paper presented at LOEX 2001: Managing Library Instruction Programs in Academic Libraries, Ypsilanti, MI, February 15, 2001).

26. Debra Gilchrist, "Improving Student Learning: Outcomes Assessment and Information Literacy Instruction" [paper presented at the ACRL/IIL Immersion, University of Colorado, Colorado Springs, 2002]).

27. Patricia Iannuzzi, "We Are Teaching, but Are They Learning: Accountability, Productivity, and Assessment," *Journal of Academic Librarianship* 25, no. 4 (July 1999): 304.

28. Megan Oakleaf, Michelle S. Millet, and Leah Kraus, "All Together Now: Getting Faculty, Administrators, and Staff Engaged in Information Literacy Assessment," *portal* 11, no. 3 (July 2011): 831–852.

Chapter Four

Library Assessment for Online, Blended, and Other Learning Environments

Maria R. Barefoot, **MLIS, AHIP**
Health Sciences Librarian
Youngstown State University
Youngstown, OH

Introduction

In 2008, the *Journal of Library Administration* reported a study that evaluated how many schools were assessing their online library education services and what methods they were using. Out of the seventy-five responses, the author found that online library services mainly consisted of the library website, online tutorials, and a direct contact librarian. Of those schools, 60 percent of the libraries did no assessment of their online services.[1] However, in 2011, the National Center for Education Statistics reported that in the 2007-2008 academic year 20.4 percent of all higher education undergraduate students were taking at least one distance education course.[2] This means that a large portion of libraries are trying to cater to the increasing demand for online education services but have no concept of how well they are actually achieving that goal.

While not all online classes are delivered to distance students, the National Center for Education Statistics uses the term *distance education* for courses that are "primarily delivered using live, interactive audio or videoconferencing, pre-recorded instructional videos, webcasts, CD-ROM or DVD, or computer-based systems delivered over the Internet."[3] In recent years, students—even those who are not distance learners—have been spending more and more time in online classes.

Libraries are in a unique position to capitalize on trends such as flipped classrooms, blended classrooms, and MOOCs. By incorporating webcasts and other online instructional tools, librarians can offer traditional instruction and also include value-added learning exercises such as supervised assignments and interactive learning. Flipped and blended classrooms capitalize on these trends by asking students to watch prerecorded lecture videos and then practice skills during class time. MOOCs utilize prerecorded lectures as well and can also include interactive tutorials to help solidify lessons.

When designing any kind of online library services, assessment must be taken into consideration at the beginning stages of the project. With library liaison work, many online services are geared toward library instruction that can include anything from a short tutorial to a fully embedded librarian in an online course. Moving to online formats can be motivated by a number of factors, such as supplementing an on-campus course, providing information literacy education in an asynchronous online course, or enabling students to learn at the point of need how to use library resources. Whatever the motivation for pursuing online library education, there are four basic criteria needed for success. Each online program developed should have

1. Clearly defined goals and objectives
2. An uncomplicated method of delivering information
3. Formative feedback from the instructor regarding the application of the information
4. Assessment procedures applied for the improvement of the course

While these steps seem linear in nature, they actually exist in a perpetual loop that involves creating and re-creating online materials according to the assessment outcomes that are defined in the goals and objectives.[4] In actual application, these steps would look like the loop in figure 4.1.

Figure 4.1
Assessment Loop

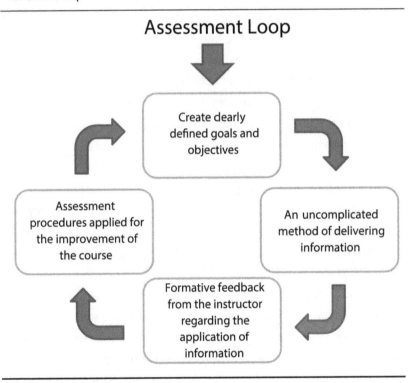

Assessment Loop

Create clearly defined goals and objectives

An uncomplicated method of delivering information

Formative feedback from the instructor regarding the application of information

Assessment procedures applied for the improvement of the course

---

Clearly defined goals and objectives are a major focus of many articles dealing with developing online library education tools. These goals create the basis for the first step of the assessment process, which dictates that one must know what to assess before moving forward. Developing clear goals and objectives allows learners to focus on what they should take away from the online tool and defines what the librarian should assess to determine the success of the tool. These goals can be directly developed into the delivery of information, formative feedback, and applied assessment stages.[5]

In order to apply the set goals, any online instruction must have some type of software for the delivery of that information. The key term in the second criterion listed above is *uncomplicated*. Many tools exist for developing online library education, but many of these tools can be cumbersome to manipulate even for college students who have grown up with technology. Mestre mentions these shortcomings in a usability study examining a screencast library tutorial. The need for easy navigation between sections was one of the main responses from students in her survey, along with the need for an easy way to work along with the tutorial, and providing different options for advanced and novice learners.[6] These details create an uncomplicated tutorial that allows the student to focus on the skills being taught and not the platform.

The platform is not the only barrier to successful online learning, however. The formative feedback mentioned in the third criterion listed above is the type of learning that contributes to students' knowledge development by asking them to apply the skills or concepts they have learned.[7] Formative feedback assumes that the student is invested in the library skills that are being presented and is willing to apply the feedback provided to the learning process. In an online environment, this type of learner dedication is crucial to the learning process because the librarian may not have the time or access to communicate with each student individually. However, Draper comments that many times, students are invested only as much as they must be to achieve a certain goal, such as passing a class with a certain grade.[8] This assumption is particularly harmful to library instruction.

Creating student investment in an online learning module is heavily reliant upon the librarian's ability to tie the lesson directly to the student's class performance or eventual grade. To achieve this level of buy-in from the student, the librarian will first have to achieve buy-in from the course instructor. This relationship is often best developed by building upon already existing relationships. For instance, the librarian can look for online courses that are being taught by instructors that the librarian has worked with in person. When the instructor is already aware of the skills the librarian can provide, he or she may be more willing to discuss adding a graded library component.

The final criterion listed above focuses on applying assessment procedures as a regular part of online learning. The formative techniques discussed above can be effective only when the library tools are regularly updated to meet the needs of the learners. The built-in quiz can tell the librarian whether the online content needs to be updated in order to increase effectiveness. However, as a mechanical learning device, effective assessment must also include information about the ease of use of the online tool. These types of assessment are often referred to as usability studies. A usability study may be conducted in two common ways. In the survey method, the learner completes a survey about various aspects of the learning tool, such as clarity and navigation. In the observation method, a learner is asked to complete the learning tool with a librarian present to view how the learner moves through the tool. In the online environment, the librarian could ask the student to report each click made as he or she moves through the online tool. If the librarian has access to screencasting software, such as Camtasia or QuickTime Pro, it would also be possible to ask the learner to record his or her interaction with the learning tool and send the video to the librarian electronically for evaluation. Whichever scenario is used, the librarian is provided with valuable information about how the online learning module is being utilized.

Reporting of Online Assessment

The steps listed above for assessing online library education provide only a small snapshot of individual online module assessment within the larger frame of how the library unit as a whole performs for distance students. To properly close the assessment loop, liaison librarians must be able to report on their online education effectiveness with a direct correlation to the metrics set forth by library administration and by the institution as a whole. This process involves both the first and fourth criteria for the assessment process mentioned in the previous section.

While the value of information literacy instruction is notoriously difficult to measure, a number of assessment outcomes can be used as benchmarking tools in this process. These outcomes include standards set by library organizations such as the Association of College and Research Libraries (ACRL) as well as national and local organizational standards. While some institutions may already have standards specific to distance and online learning in place, others may not.[9] In these instances, it is prudent to develop assessment standards that incorporate national guidelines while staying within the goals of the local institution.

For instance, national ACRL standards for distance library education suggest creating local goals and objectives for online students by

- [incorporating] the distance learning mission statement, goals, and objectives into those of the library and of the originating institution as a whole
- [involving] the distance learning community representatives, including local administrators and on-site faculty and students, in the formation of the objectives and the regular evaluation of their achievement[10]

ACRL provides some sample outcomes that relate specifically to online learning for Performance Indicator 3.3 of the *Standards for Libraries in Higher Education*:

Library personnel model best pedagogical practices for classroom teaching, online tutorial design, and other educational practices:

- Students evaluate classes given by librarians as effective and interesting.
- Students rate online tutorials as educational and engaging.
- Faculty value librarian input on teaching and learning techniques.[11]

These standards are well known within the library community but are often left out of the planning for assessment within an institution. The Council for the Advancement of Standards in Higher Education provides a standard tool for institution-wide initiatives in a university setting. These standards contain a section dedicated to library services for distance education, which states, "Library services should include online tutorials on conducting library research."[12]

These standards, while important, can be very broadly interpreted. Unfortunately, none of these national goals and objectives provides much in the way of actual numbers or metrics that liaison librarians can use to document their efforts. White noticed this confusion when he found that within the library literature, assessment is almost always focused inward and does not involve many of the common library stakeholders, such as administrators, students, and faculty.[13] He also noticed that while most library assessment is qualitative in nature, it does little to address the real quantitative factors, such as financial value added to the student experience. These initial goals are key to maintaining an ongoing effective library presence in online environments, as mentioned earlier.

Aligning the assessment of individual liaison efforts with those of the larger institution can provide meaningful data to the larger institution. Therefore, it is absolutely essential that online library education be tied to some of the most important assessment data at a higher education institution: graduation rates, GPA/QPA, and time to program completion. In order to align online library education with the higher goals of the institution, the librarian must begin by moving traditional paper-based assessment tools into the online environment. The University of Maryland University College (UMUC) succeeded both in migrating a traditional in-person course to an online course and in aligning its assessment methods to match those of the larger university institution.[14] By moving the non–credit-bearing library introduction course to a required credit-bearing online course, UMUC was able to create an online information literacy education experience that was meaningful both to the students and to the institution. Its course goals and objectives were aligned with the American Library Association national standards for information literacy and were assessed with a pretest and posttest, research log, and course participation. UMUC was also able to close the assessment loop by evaluating the course with student surveys and making major course revisions every two to three years.

This example elaborates on the necessity of assessment standards that provide information about student learning while still providing an application to institutional reporting measures, such as grades and student achievements. Unfortunately, not every library has the support to develop effective tools such as those above. However, simple methods, such as working with faculty to include graded research portfolios, bibliographies, or other assignment in information literacy courses can have a larger impact when reported consistently to library and university administrators.[15] By setting specific goals for online library programs, assessing programs according to those goals, and then reporting assessment outcomes to the administration, librarians can make library education an essential part of the online learning process.

Software Restraints and Benefits

The development of online library education and reporting of assessment outcomes are both reliant upon and constrained by the software that is used to implement them. The second criterion for successful online assessment focuses on the technical skills needed for successful online learning. For this discussion, one must return to the idea of what needs to be assessed. In many instances, librarians must assess student learning in order to determine if their online presence was successful, but in the online environment one must also consider the overall usability of the learning tools that were implemented.

Certain software, such as course management systems, is intended to deal with assessment of student learning. These systems, such as WebCT, Blackboard, Moodle, and many others, are often utilized by an entire institution. These systems are often trumpeted as ways to either enhance courses or provide course content completely free of time restrictions. However, many faculty members and students have reported that course management systems often require more time for course development, reading, and working through the material provided.[16] One thing they do provide is easy integration with already existing campus software. When a library assessment tool is developed in the existing management system, it is more likely that the students will already be familiar with the software, thus making it easier to use.

Blackboard is one of the most widely discussed management systems where librarians have been able to develop a presence. In order to conduct assessment of library skills within Blackboard, the literature reports on two common methods: the librarian being embedded within an existing course as a support person or the library adding relevant online content that can be applied to any course. The embedded method was used by Markgraf, who utilized the varying roles that can be assigned to a Blackboard user. She noted that when she was assigned an instructor role instead of a student role, she was granted access to statistics such as the number of times a post had been read and the number of students accessing it at varying times of day on both an aggregate and individual student level.[17]

The "library as an entity" approach was taken by the librarians at Brooklyn College Library. In their assessment techniques, they were able to implement pretests and posttests using multiple-choice and matching questions and then export the aggregate data. While this did provide a way to assess student learning of the library modules, it was not as versatile as the librarians had hoped. Specific problems included the inability to randomize questions according to topic and the inability mix open-ended questions with other question types, such as multiple-choice. It also did not allow the export of data on individual questions, only on the entire quiz result.[18] These shortcomings are all common complaints about the limitations of many learning management systems in assessing student learning.

The other side of online assessment falls to the usability of librarian-developed tools, which often include tutorials, websites, and apps. Assessment of these tools can help determine where changes of a technical nature can be made to improve the performance of the student. Some of the major areas of a usability study focus on the ease of student or faculty adoption of a new technology, the time that is required for a student to move through the learning module, and the incorporation of multiple learning styles.

The software chosen for the development of an online learning tool is directly related to the final usability. For instance, when developing an online learning module that is easy for a student or faculty member to adopt, the librarian must consider the available controls in the final product. Some features that are often listed as ideal for online learning environments include the ability of a student to see a navigation panel in the learning module. This feature usually allows the student to move around within the tutorial in order to focus on places where he or she has the most difficulty. This freedom to navigate is available in a number of software programs, including learning management systems like Blackboard and the free web-based course management software Udutu.[19]

Most learners utilize one or two senses more strongly than the others to help them learn effectively. The kinesthetic learner absorbs information more easily through physical movement, the visual learner through visual aids, and the auditory learner through sound. The ability to navigate freely is probably best suited to students with a kinesthetic learning style who are accustomed to common website navigations. However, there are many student learners whose learning styles focus more on auditory or visual learning and may not be as familiar with website navigation.

These students may have an easier time using a tutorial that is visually based, which can be created using many of the screencasting software programs available. Camtasia and Prezi include many audiovisual tools, such as screencasting and zooming. They also offer an audio element for students who learn better by hearing.

One feature that is essential to any learning style is a manageable time frame for completing the library module. Many students are overwhelmed with reading and other work in an online learning environment, which moves them to focus on using the library information only if necessary, often as reference material to help complete their assignments. In these instances, librarians have often attempted to make videos very short, teaching only one or two concepts, or have relied upon the student's ability to jump around in a learning module to review the pieces needed.

A usability assessment can help identify places for improvement in technical design. In a usability assessment, the students are often asked to use the learning tool, then reflect upon their experience. One excellent usability study was conducted at the University of Illinois at Urbana-Champaign. This study asked that students take a learning assessment questionnaire to determine their preferred learning style, then had the students work through the tutorials and recorded their movements.[20] This method of assessment may need to be adapted for the online environment by employing an online survey tool such as SurveyMonkey. In these instances, it may be useful to ask the students to complete the tutorial, then respond to questions about the ease of use of the tutorial. It is also important to include relevant links to the tutorial within the online survey for clarity. Studying the usability of online library materials allows the librarian to maintain a well-built online learning module, as dictated by the second criterion for effective online library assessment.

Special Issues in Online Environments

Assessing learning in an online environment comes with many challenges for providing feedback that are not presented in physical learning venues. For instance, online learning tools are usually asynchronous. Thus, students must either wait for feedback from the librarian or rely on immediate computerized feedback. Delayed feedback is more closely related to the assessment methods that are common in the physical learning environment, where students must turn in assignments then wait for them to be graded and returned. Delayed feedback in an online environment usually includes direct communication with the librarian via electronic methods, such as e-mail or through a course management system. It enables the librarian to give individual attention to the research needs of each student and to create the kind of formative feedback that increases knowledge retention. It is also one of the only methods that can employ open-ended answers from students, allowing them to use their own words.

Markgraf used delayed feedback regularly as a part of her role as an embedded librarian.[21] Her communication tactics included e-mail and message boards within the Blackboard system. The assessment tactic she employed during this class was to compare the final grades of students who had communicated with the librarian with those who had not. The results showed a correlation between higher grades and librarian interaction, even though these students had delayed access to librarian feedback. Though this correlation does not prove that the librarian's role caused the students to achieve higher grades, this type of anecdotal evidence can provide an argument for increased library services to online students.

While forms of delayed feedback can be more conducive to student learning, they are much harder to assess for documentation and reporting purposes on a large scale. Responding to message board postings and individual e-mails requires an exceptional amount of time on the part of the librarian and also requires time-consuming documenting procedures. In order to report on these interactions, the librarian must keep a record of each student who communicated and compare those students with those who did not.

Some relief from this documentation process involves automating feedback so that it can be delivered immediately. These types of feedback are often administered in the form of quizzes, pre-surveys, post-surveys, or a combination of these tools. Many online learning tools now offer quizzes that can be graded automatically or that provide a response to the students as they practice. These types of automated learning are beneficial for assessment reporting because the data can be easily collected and distributed to management authorities. This type of data collection can also help address one of the barriers preventing MOOCs, or massive open online courses, from becoming an official learning method that is recognized by both employers and academic institutions.[22] Assessment is crucial in verifying whether a person has acquired the necessary knowledge to receive academic credit, and by collecting automatic feedback, learners can prove they have achieved the necessary level of learning. In MOOCs with large student enrollments, this is possibly the only feasible way to provide assessment.

However, automated feedback in student learning relies heavily on the student's dedication to the task at hand. Many students are only as invested in learning library skills as is related to their completion of a course.[23] This was also observed during an online class where the students were not required to view the library materials provided.[24] This means that students may move through an automated learning module without really reading the feedback that is presented to them or applying it to their own learning. Some suggestions for keeping students engaged with automated feedback include making learning modules more interactive by including audio, visual, and kinesthetic learning devices. Linking to short learning modules within assignments and other contextually relevant locations can also improve student engagement with the information literacy learning process.[25]

The automated learning environment provides another debate in the arena of assessment outcomes. In the automated learning modules listed above, and in some newer learning models such as MOOCs, the students are often expected to assess their own work. This type of learning and assessment requires not only that the student is dedicated enough to self-teach, but also that the instructor creates a module that can stand alone with no instructor involvement. This is absolutely essential for any MOOC course where anyone in the world can access the course at any time. But even in traditional online education environments, librarians often face this same scenario where they must reach thousands of students without individual contact.

MOOCs and online learning environments with few librarians often must rely completely on question formats that have designated answers, such as multiple-choice, matching, etc. Open-ended responses often require more thought from students, but automating feedback for open-response questions is a difficult task. There has been some advancement in assessing open-response questions with automated systems. One such system is the OpenMark system, developed at the Open University, which offers feedback to each open-response question and allows students to change their answers based on that feedback. This system can also be used in graded assessment by decreasing the points awarded with each incorrect attempt.[26] These types of systems, while in their infancy, can provide a tool for librarians attempting to provide information literacy education to online students. Creating library modules that employ formative learning techniques, as mentioned in the third criterion of the assessment loop, can provide a concrete method of measuring the impact of online library education on learning.

Conclusion

As the demand for online learning continues to rise, institutions of higher education will require increasing participation from libraries and librarians. This environment demands that librarians learn to assess their online activities in a way that is meaningful for the library and for the larger institutions that they serve. Doing so may involve working with other university departments that are focused on online learning. Many universities have a department dedicated to online programs that can help in developing online assessment tools. Contacting specific program directors who are responsible for their own online programs may be another option for librarians looking to create or improve their online assessment methods. These university contacts are a valuable resource in creating assessment-oriented online programs and including library assessment materials in existing outcome measurements.

For any librarian developing online assessment, the focus must be placed on the learning goals, structured with delayed or immediate feedback, and then reported using measurements already respected by the university community. The education literature and local curriculum committees can provide a wealth of information for online curriculum design and reporting standards. The inclusion of library services in online education relies on librarians who meticulously create educational materials and routinely report on those findings to their administration. The assessment loop discussed above provides this framework for successful online library education.

Notes

1. Samantha Schmehl Hines, "How It's Done: Examining Distance Education Library Instruction and Assessment," *Journal of Library Administration* 48, no. 3–4 (2008): 471, doi:10.1080/01930820802289565.

2. National Center for Education Statistics, "Fast Facts: Distance Learning," last modified 2011, http://nces.ed.gov/fastfacts/display.asp?id=80.

3. Alexandria Walton Radford, *Learning at a Distance: Undergraduate Enrollment in Distance Education Courses and Degree Programs*, Stats in Brief, NCES 2012-154 (Washington, DC: US Department of Education, October, 2011), 19, http://nces.ed.gov/pubs2012/2012154.pdf.

4. Bonnie J. M. Swoger, "Closing the Assessment Loop Using Pre- and Post-assessment," *Reference Services Review* 39, no. 2 (May 2011): 244, doi:10.1108/00907321111135475.

5. Ligaya A. Ganster and Tiffany R. Walsh, "Enhancing Library Instruction to Undergraduates: Incorporating Online Tutorials into the Curriculum," *College and Undergraduate Libraries* 15, no. 3 (June 2008): 319, doi:10.1080/10691310802258232.

6. Lori S. Mestre, "Student Preference for Tutorial Design: A Usability Study," *Reference Services Review* 40, no. 2 (May 2012): 271–272, doi:10.1108/00907321211228318.

7. Judy Block, "Distance Education Library Services Assessment," *E-JASL: The Electronic Journal of Academic and Special Librarianship* 9, no. 3 (Winter 2008), http://southernlibrarianship.icaap.org/content/v09n03/block_j01.html.

8. Stephen W. Draper, "What Are Learners Actually Regulating When Given Feedback?" BJET: *British Journal of Educational Technology* 40, no. 2 (March 2009): 307, doi:10.1111/j.1467-8535.2008.00930.x.

9. Karen Sobel and Kenneth Wolf, "Updating Your Tool Belt: Redesigning Assessments of Learning in the Library," *Reference and User Services Quarterly* 50, no. 3 (Spring 2011): 246–247.

10. Association of College and Research Libraries, *Standards for Distance Learning Library Services* (Chicago: Association of College and Research Libraries, July 1, 2008), www.ala.org/acrl/standards/guidelinesdistancelearning.

11. Association of College and Research Libraries, "Appendix 1: Sample Outcomes," *Standards for Libraries in Higher Education* (Chicago: Association of College and Research Libraries, October 2011), www.ala.org/acrl/standards/slhe2.

12. Laura A Dean, ed., *CAS Professional Standards for Higher Education*, 7th ed. (Washington, DC: Council for the Advancement of Standards in Higher Education, 2009), 214.

13. Larry Nash White, "Assessment Planning for Distance Education Library Services: Strategic Roadmaps for Determining and Reporting Organizational Performance and Value," *Journal of Library Administration* 50, no. 7/8 (October 2010): 1018–1019, doi:10.1080/01930826.2010.489007.

14. Elizabeth Mulherrin, Kimberly B. Kelley, and Diane Fishman, "Information Literacy and the Distant Student: One University's Experience Developing, Delivering, and Maintaining an Online, Required Information Literacy Course," *Internet Reference Services Quarterly* 9, no. 1/2 (January 2004): 34–35, doi:10.1300/J136v09n01_03.

15. Bryna Coonin and Angela Whitehurst, "The Assessment Portfolio: A Possible Answer to the Distance Education Assessment Dilemma," *Internet Reference Services Quarterly* 16, no. 3 (July 2011): 94–95, doi:10.1080/10875301.2011.595216.

16. Susan Gibbons, "Course-Management Systems," *Library Technology Reports* 41, no. 3 (May 2005): 11.

17. Jill S. Markgraf, "Librarian Participation in the Online Classroom," *Internet Reference Services Quarterly* 9, no. 1/2 (January 2004): 11, doi:10.1300/J136v09n01_02.

18. Maura A. Smale and Mariana Regalado, "Using Blackboard to Deliver Library Research Skills Assessment," *Communications in Information Literacy* 3, no. 2 (September 2009): 152.

19. Maria R. Barefoot, "Creating Interactive Library Tutorials," *MLA News* 53, no. 4 (April 2013): 21.

20. Mestre, "Student Preference for Tutorial Design," 262–263.

21. Markgraf, "Librarian Participation in the Online Classroom," 13.

22. Brandi Scardilli, "MOOCs: Classes for the Masses," *Information Today* 30, no. 8 (September 2013): 32–34.

23. Draper, "What Are Learners Actually Regulating?" 307.

24. Mary Edwards, Swapna Kumar, and Marilyn Ochoa, "Assessing the Value of Embedded Librarians in an Online Graduate Educational Technology Course," *Public Services Quarterly* 6, no. 2–3 (January 1, 2010): 285, doi:10.1080/15228959.2010.497447.

25. B. Jane Scales et al., "If You Build It, Will They Learn? Assessing Online Information Literacy Tutorials." *College and Research Libraries* 67, no. 5 (September 2006): 443.

26. Sally Jordan and Tom Mitchell, "E-Assessment for Learning? The Potential of Short-Answer Free-Text Questions with Tailored Feedback," *BJET: British Journal of Educational Technology* 40, no. 2 (March 1, 2009): 376, doi:10.1111/j.1467-8535.2008.00928.x.

Chapter Five

Beyond the Bibliographer

Assessing Collection Development Activities in the New Digital Library

Daniel C. Mack
Associate Dean for Collection Strategies and Services
University of Maryland Libraries
College Park, MD

Collection development librarians face both enormous challenges and exciting opportunities in the early twenty-first century. Technological advances continue to alter dramatically how libraries acquire, deliver, and manage their collections. Trends in scholarship, including the increasingly interdisciplinary and international nature of curricula and the research enterprise, play an ever-growing role in the collections that librarians develop for their institutions. And possibly most important of all, collection development in the academy is no longer a stand-alone activity, divorced from the other services that libraries offer to their users. Because collections and the librarians who work with them are in a state of flux, libraries must reexamine how they assess the work of collection development. Increasingly, these endeavors are not just about assessing collections. Rather, they are increasingly concerned with assessing people's work: the effort, expertise, and time that liaison librarians devote not only to developing collections, but also to integrating these collections into other library services.

Because of these changes in collections, librarians must transform the way they do collection development in the academy. At most institutions the day is long since past when bibliographers sat in offices in the back of the stacks, surrounded by publishers' catalogs and occasionally consulting with faculty. Today's collection development librarian usually performs several functions, including providing services for reference and research consultation, bibliographic instruction, consultation on issues such as copyright and open access, and outreach. Many are subject specialists with a disciplinary background and serve as liaisons to specific academic departments and programs. Collection development is only one of many activities, and librarians must integrate collection work into their comprehensive program of services. All of this means that libraries must change the way that they assess collections and those who develop and manage then. The most transformational change that libraries need is to start assessing collection development activities, and not just collections. In other words, libraries should examine not only what librarians collect, but also how and why they collect what they do.

Libraries have long gathered, analyzed, and made decisions based on collection data, including counts of volumes and titles held, numbers of downloads and turnaways for subscribed online content, and dollars spent by disciplinary area and format. These and other metrics for library collections are important, and libraries should certainly continue to keep and use such data. However, what has often been lacking is documentation regarding how librarians with collection development responsibilities create the collections that these numbers describe. So the library needs to ask, what activities do our librarians do to develop and maintain collections that support the curricular and research needs of our users? The *Guidelines for Liaison Work in Managing Collections and Services* from the Reference and User Services Association (RUSA) identifies several activities, including creating and publicizing collection development policies, identifying appropriate types and levels of service for individual constituencies, and various engagement and outreach activities to those constituencies.[1] Many, if not most, of these activities, involve collections.

In addition to the outreach, engagement, and other liaison work that occupy many collection development librarians' time, other factors have dramatically changed the work of collection development and management itself. Librarians now spend an increasing amount of time doing more than just identifying content for their collections. Information technology, academic publishing, and user demand will continue to evolve, creating new problems that collection development librarians must solve. These include addressing trends like the move from print to digital and from ownership to access, as well as solutions for issues such as copyright, fair use, open access. In addition, libraries function within an ever-expanding environment of partnerships for shared print repositories, consortial acquisition and licensing, and other cooperative collection development programs. Finally, all of these factors continue to unfold in a climate of increasing budget constraints and demands for accountability in higher education.

Lewis identifies a handful of key trends facing academic library collections in the next several years. These include deconstructing legacy print collections, moving toward on-demand acquisitions, facilitating open-access journals, curating unique content, and creating new ways to fund national infrastructure to support access to and curation of digital collections.[2] These developments identify some of the primary emerging collection development activities that librarians must now incorporate into their efforts and for which they must also devise new metrics, means of documentation, and assessment measures. In brief, collection development assessment efforts must undergo a fundamental shift from not only measuring the collection, to also evaluating librarians' work as they interact with the collection.

In addition to the traditional role of selecting subject-based content, new and developing processes that now occupy much of the time and effort of liaison librarians with collection development responsibilities therefore fall into two general categories. First are those that are related to the expanding role of liaison librarians in the intellectual life of the academy. This category includes reference and research consultation, bibliographic instruction, support for MOOCs and other online education, and other forms of engagement with faculty, students, and other library users. It also includes creating and promoting policies to govern and coordinate these activities. Librarians engaging in these actions are focused outward from the library collection and toward the various constituencies they serve. While this work does not directly develop or manage library collections, is does (or ought to) inform librarians' collection development efforts. A considerable amount of liaison outreach focuses on instructing users in identifying and accessing content and in integrating the results into their research. Combining this with digital collections and Internet-based modes of interaction, the liaison librarian has evolved into a hybrid construct of bibliographer, reference librarian, and instructor in a model that Yoder calls the "cyborg librarian."[3]

This category of increased interaction with the academy also includes issues over which librarians may have little control but must nevertheless find solutions. Chief among these challenges are unstable and insufficient collections budgets, outdated and overcrowded library facilities, and collections managed in an increasingly collaborative environment in conjunction with consortia and other partners. Liaison librarians increasingly find that they must participate in analyzing these issues, creating solutions for them, and then implementing these solutions. While collection development librarians have long been accustomed to managing budgets, serials inflation, and other fiscal matters, they must now deal on the one hand with budgets that are often significantly behind the rate of inflation, and on the other hand with new models of pricing and funding, including demand-driven acquisition and the huge issue of access over ownership. In addition, most academic libraries now face both internal and external pressure to repurpose library spaces. Because libraries often occupy valuable real estate on campus, and because the use of print and other analog collections continues to decline, most libraries have at least begun to plan for ways in which they can store or deaccession underused print collections to create technology-rich, collaborative user spaces. Off-site storage and shared print repositories can offer solutions, and creating these solutions requires the expertise of liaison librarians. In the increasingly collaborative environment of academic libraries, liaison librarians must now often work with consortial and other external partners to solve both budgetary and space problems.

The second category of issues with which collection development librarians must grapple are those related to the changes in information technology and academic publishing. New models for distributing, acquiring, and accessing information continue to influence collection development. Topics such as open-source publishing, e-book functionality, digital rights management (DRM), licensing of copyrighted materials, and access to and storage of online content challenge liaison librarians. The work of collection development has always required librarians to remain up-to-date on publishing trends. In the past, these trends have traditionally been primarily focused on content, such as knowing which publishers focus on specific disciplines and audiences. Now and in the future, librarians responsible for collections must also understand the technology that impacts how digital collections are acquired, discovered, and curated. In addition to this, academic publishing has become increasingly interdisciplinary and international, which reflects the trend in university-sponsored research across all subject areas.

Liaison librarians with responsibilities for collection development must therefore take new approaches to how they assess their work. This assessment cannot focus only on the content of collections. Rather, it must now also include assessing the work that liaison librarians do to fund collections in often tight budget circumstances, acquire and make accessible digital collections with a wide variety of access and functionality models, solve problems relating to space for and storage of physical collections, and integrate collection development into the other services that they offer their constituencies. A collection development assessment program for liaison librarians should therefore address the following elements:

- disciplinary content of collections
- information technology and new modes for acquisition and delivery of content

- budgeting, development, and stewardship
- format, space, preservation, and curation of collections in all formats
- integration of collection development into instruction, research assistance, and other engagement with the academic community

How can liaison librarians identify, document, and assess collection development work in these categories? The RUSA *Guidelines for Liaison Work in Managing Collections and Services* mentioned above offer a useful starting point for identifying areas to assess.[4] Other recent works provide specific assessment measures that are directly relevant to these categories. Nagra reviews a wide range of metrics that liaison librarians can use to measure and assess library collections.[5] Sutton offers another model geared toward the value of digital resources.[6] Trail, Chang-FitzGibbon, and Wishnetsky present an assessment tool specifically for cutting serials from the collections budget.[7] These tools present librarians with a range of options, depending on specific circumstances, from which to draw assessment measures relating to collection development, budgeting, and use.

Other recent literature offers some insight into how liaison librarians can assess the integration of collection development into their other engagement and outreach efforts with the various audiences they serve. As Carpan demonstrates, building user-focused collections requires development of strong relationships with faculty.[8] Malenfant presents a case study from the University of Minnesota that offers a model for engaging liaison librarians with collegiate faculty.[9] Cooke et al. provide a framework for assessing liaison librarians' impact on their constituencies.[10] Recent literature also emphasizes the need for incorporating both quantitative and qualitative assessment into collection development programs. Sfakakis and Kapidakis offer models for incorporating metrics into the assessment and evaluation of digital content and offer suggestions for making data-driven decisions about digital research collections.[11] Behr and Hill demonstrate how assessment, especially data-driven quantitative measures, can provide important information to drive decisions about collection content and focus.[12] Blake and Schleper discuss how assessment can inform the creation of a complete collection development program.[13] Wisneski writes about the need for a programmatic approach to develop the skills of new collections librarians and offers a framework for creating such a program.[14] This body of research offers librarians a range of tools for assessing their work with library collections, as well as documenting the positive impact that their collection development activities have on their other efforts as liaison librarians.

An assessment program for academic libraries in the twenty-first century must therefore incorporate tools for evaluating activities under specific rubrics. Both data and narrative information are crucial to collection development assessment because these activities require both qualitative and quantitative measures. The table below provides a model for developing a basic assessment program for collection development that can be modified for specific librarians, institutions, and circumstances.

Developing outstanding academic library collections increasingly demands that librarians keep apace not only with the trends that influence the disciplinary content of collections, but also with ongoing developments in academic research and publishing, information technology, innovative models for accessing and delivering collections, and issues of space, format, and budgeting. However, in the twenty-first-century academic library, even excellence in collection development is not sufficient for liaison librarians. The best collections in the world are useless if they are not integrated into a robust suite of liaison activities, including reference and research assistance, library instruction, and other outreach and engagement activities with students, faculty, and other researchers. A forward-thinking program of collection assessment will offer liaison librarians a wide range of tools, from which they can select those that are relevant to their specific positions. These tools consist of use metrics and financial figures that support data-driven decisions, as well as narratives and other qualitative measures that document the effect that library collections have on the institution. Liaison librarians with collection development responsibilities can employ such a user-focused assessment

Table 5.1
Assessing Collection Development Activities

Type of Activity	Specific Activities	Assessment Measures and Documentation
Disciplinary Content	• Discuss curricular and research priorities with collegiate faculty • Follow new courses and programs approved by institution • Track use of materials by subject area • Create user guides to collection content • Participate in program reaccreditation projects	• Reports of acquisitions that support new curriculum and research initiatives • Collections usage data and circulation counts • Track number of sessions and attendance of meetings with collegiate faculty to discuss collections support for research and teaching • Data on number and use of guides • Accreditation reports • Reports for University, college and departmental curriculum committees
Access, Distribution and Publishing Trends	• Investigate and implement demand driven acquisition and other new and emerging models of distribution and access • Stay current on new publishing trends • Inform collegiate faculty of new access and distribution models	• Usage data for demand driven acquisitions • Dollar amount and percentage of budget spend on demand driven acquisition • Track number of sessions and attendance of meetings with collegiate faculty to discuss publishing, access and distribution
Fiscal and Development Issues	• Spend gift funds and endowments according to purpose of gift • Track spending by subject area • Track spending by format and material type • Follow established fiscal calendar	• Dollar amount and percentage of budget spent by subject area and format • Stewardship reports to apprise donors and other stakeholders of collections
Physical Collections, Space and Formats	• Eliminate unnecessary duplication across formats and locations • Weed physical content that does not support current and future curriculum and research enterprise • Collaborate with collegiate faculty to identify appropriate formats and material types for disciplinary areas	• Track number of titles and items withdrawn • Report on amount of space saved for new collections and for repurposing • Data on collection migration from analog to digital formats by discipline
Policy Creation	• Create subject-specific collection policies • Create policies to address format, duplication and space • Create policies to address demand driven acquisition, access vs. ownership and other new and emerging models of access and distribution	• Track number of policies created • Report on how policy creation supports other collection activities above

program to demonstrate that their work to create relevant library collections has a positive impact on the experience of library users and makes a difference in the intellectual and cultural life of the academy.

Notes

1.   Liaison with Users Committee, *Guidelines for Liaison Work in Managing Collections and Services* (Chicago: Reference and User Services Association, 1992, rev. 2001), www.ala.org/rusa/resources/guidelines/guidelinesliaison.

2.   David W. Lewis, "From Stacks to the Web: The Transformation of Academic Library Collecting," *College and Research Libraries* 74, no. 2 (March 2013): 168–172.

3.   Amanda R. Yoder, "The Cyborg Librarian as Interface: Interpreting Postmodern Discourse on Knowledge Construction, Validation, and Navigation within Academic Libraries," *portal: Libraries and the Academy* 3, no. 3 (July 2003): 381–392.

4.   Liaison with Users Committee, *Guidelines for Liaison Work.*

5.   Kanu A. Nagra, "The Evaluation of Use of Electronic Resources and Services in Academic Libraries: A Study of E-metrics and Related Methods for Measurement and Assessment," *Journal of Library Administration and Management Section (JLAMS)* 6, no. 1 (September 2009): 28–41.

6.   Sarah Sutton, "A Model for Electronic Resources Value Assessment," *Serials Librarian* 64, no. 1–4 (2013): 245–253, doi:10.1080/0361526X.2013.760417.

7.   Mary Ann Trail, Kerry Chang-FitzGibbon, and Susan Wishnetsky, "Using Assessment to Make Difficult Choices in Cutting Periodicals," *Serials Librarian* 62, no. 1–4 (2012): 159–163, doi:10.1080/0361526X.2012.652931.

8.   Carolyn Carpan, "The Importance of Library Liaison Programs," *College and Undergraduate Libraries* 18, no. 1 (2011): 104–110, doi:10.1080/10691316.2011.550536.

9.   Kara J. Malenfant, "Leading Change in the System of Scholarly Communication: A Case Study of Engaging Liaison Librarians for Outreach to Faculty," *College and Research Libraries* 71, no. 1 (January 2010): 63–76.

10. Louise Cooke et al., "Evaluating the Impact of Academic Liaison Librarians on Their User Community: A Review and Case Study," *New Review of Academic Librarianship* 17, no. 1 (2011): 5–30, doi:10.1080/13614533.2011.539096.

11. Michalis Sfakakis and Sarantos Kapidakis, "User Behavior Tendencies on Data Collections in a Digital Library," in *Research and Advanced Technology for Digital Libraries: 6th European Conference, ECDL 2002, Rome, Italy, September 2002, Proceedings*, ed. Maristella Agosti and Costantino Thanos, Lecture Notes in Computer Science 2458 (Berlin: Springer, 2002): 550–559.

12. Michele Behr and Rebecca Hill, "Mining e-Reserves Data for Collection Assessment: An Analysis of How Instructors Use Library Collections to Support

Distance Learners," *Journal of Library & Information Services in Distance Learning 6, no. 3–4 (2012): 159–179.*

13. Julie C. Blake and Susan P. Schleper, "From Data to Decisions: Using Surveys and Statistics to Make Collection Management Decisions," *Library Collections, Acquisitions, and Technical Services* 28, no. 4, (Winter 2004): 460–464.

14. Richard Wisneski, "Collection Development Assessment for New Collection Development Librarians," *Collection Management* 33, no. 1–22 (2008): 143–159.

Chapter Six

Liaison Librarians and Scholarly Communication

A Framework and Strategies for Assessment

Dawn Childress
Kalin Librarian for Technological Innovation in the Humanities
Humanities Librarian
The Pennsylvania State University Libraries
State College, PA

Daniel Hickey
Assistant Director
Hospitality, Labor, and Management Library
Cornell University Library
Ithaca, NY

Introduction

Many liaison librarians are expanding and embracing new roles and modes of engagement as scholarly communication issues become increasingly relevant to the research and teaching communities they support. Consequently, liaisons have become practiced in a wide range of scholarly communication issues and services. Still, it is unclear just how liaison librarians are participating in scholarly communication initiatives within their institution or discipline, how frequently and programmatically liaisons record and evaluate their contributions to these efforts, and what measures, if any, lend themselves to evaluating such activities. In this chapter, the authors survey the library literature, liaison resources, and a variety of librarian perspectives to better understand current practices and to identify issues related to these evolving areas of engagement. The chapter concludes by presenting a framework with which liaisons might evaluate their contributions.

Some might question the levels at which liaison librarians are expected to engage in scholarly communication activities amid the multiplicity of roles for which they are already responsible, and correspondingly the need for such assessment. However, more and more liaisons find the work they do with scholarly communication rewarding and a natural part of their liaison duties. With increasing emphasis on assessment and documentation in libraries, it is obvious that assessment measures are needed to better understand librarian contributions, but beyond this, assessment of scholarly communication activities can empower liaisons to formalize their role in this area and take ownership of their contributions.

A Review of the Literature

A review of current literature reveals that little research has been done on assessing the scholarly communication activities of liaison librarians. Still, in recent years there has been an increase in literature on liaison librarian roles and futures related to scholarly communication. In 2009, ARL released the "Special Issue on Liaison Librarian Roles" with several articles highlighting opportunities and challenges for liaison librarians in scholarly communication contexts.[1] In this issue, Kirchner identifies liaison librarians as key stakeholders in helping libraries engage with their community and better understand scholarly communication activities within their disciplines.[2] She outlines a liaison training program with several goals in mind: raise liaison awareness of new modes of scholarly communication and encourage confidence in developing service models to facilitate community participation in these new modes. Offering a liaison's perspective, Whatley advocates for building on traditional liaison roles while balancing newer ones.[3] She underscores the importance of the relationship-building aspects of liaison work and regards this as a key component of engaging with the community around new modes of scholarly communication.

Expanding on the theme of liaison roles and responsibilities related to scholarly communication, a 2012 Research Libraries UK report uncovers the skills gap of librarians in effectively supporting the evolving information needs of today's researchers.[4] The report identifies nine key areas for liaison engagement, over half of which fall under the aegis of scholarly communication. While the report finds that many liaisons, regardless of their length of service in librarianship, need substantial reskilling to effectively support new modes of research, it asserts that training in scholarly communication is the most easily available.[5]

An example of the reskilling concept can be seen in recent publications that explore the intersection between scholarly communication and the relatively well-established body of literature commenting on information literacy. Two recent publications marry the concepts to great effect. *Common Ground at the Nexus of Information Literacy and Scholarly Communication*, edited by Davis-Kahl and Hensley, is a collection of writings that suggests the integration of scholarly communication concepts into librarians' information literacy practice to achieve synergy.[6] It features a chapter by Abigail Goben with a practical application from a liaison perspective. A white paper coming out of the Association of College and Research Libraries (ACRL)'s Working Group on Intersections of Scholarly Communication and Information Literacy provides a useful meditation on that subject, putting forward four key recommendations: (1) Integrate pedagogy and scholarly communication into educational programs for librarians to achieve the ideal of information fluency; (2) develop new model information literacy curricula, incorporating evolutions in pedagogy and scholarly communication issues; (3) explore options for organizational change; and (4) promote advocacy.[7] The working group's ambitious recommendations suggest that the recent groundswell of interest in integrating scholarly communication topics and learning outcomes into core liaison job responsibilities (such as library instruction) will "help make libraries resilient in the face of the changing scholarly information environment."[8]

There are also specific areas, such as data curation and institutional repositories, where the import of a liaison's role, as opposed to that of a general librarian, has been scrutinized. Gabridge stresses the role of subject liaisons regarding STEM data curation, how a deep understanding of "the research needs of individual researchers and of the institution as a whole is a major component" of their work.[9] These insights form a conceptual and literal buttress for a data curation framework. Similarly, Newton, Miller, and Stowell Bracke expand this notion, stating that collections "destined to populate an institutional data repository are identified not in catalogs and through vendor profiles but through conversations, liaison relationships, and other professional collaborations."[10] As the key role of the liaison in scholarly communication efforts is further defined in such papers, the profession can begin to quantify and qualify liaisons' impact as well as the value they contribute through their knowledge, actions, and stewarded relationships. The insight that liaisons are uniquely qualified as partners in the process of scholarly communication permeates the literature. Systematically assessing those who are already actualizing their potential is the next step.

Research Design

To better understand the current landscape of liaison librarian scholarly communication activities and to determine if and how these activities are being assessed, the authors conducted exploratory interviews with academic librarians from a range of institutions. Libraries were selected based on available evidence of (1) emerging models of liaison participation in scholarly communication services, (2) liaison librarians who are visibly active in some aspect of scholarly communication issues, or (3) institution high profile in scholarly communication issues. Where possible, at least two librarians from each institution were interviewed, a scholarly communication librarian or similar position and a subject library head, to help ensure a balanced perspective. Scholarly communication librarians provide a broad perspective from outside the disciplinary concerns; they are in a unique position to observe the collaborations at play within the organization and to offer suggestions on the roles that liaison librarians can adopt to better address unmet user needs. On the other hand, subject library heads have direct experience overseeing liaison librarians and their own experiences as liaisons. As supervisors, they observe how liaisons within their department are engaging in scholarly communication activities and any assessment practices taking place; as liaison librarians themselves, they are acutely aware of the issues faced by incorporating scholarly communication activities into an already full workflow and of the challenges of assessing liaison activities. The librarians interviewed represent a variety of major disciplinary areas: humanities, social sciences, STEM, business, and education.

Sixteen librarians at nine institutions were contacted via e-mail to participate in the study and, after they consented to participate, phone interviews were scheduled. Interviews lasted thirty to forty-five minutes, and investigators took notes from the conversations, which were based on the same nine questions. Investigators asked follow-up questions as needed. Questions focused on the following: (1) areas, focus, and trends in scholarly communication; (2) the range and types of scholarly communication activities in which liaison librarians are participating; (3) if and how these activities are being tracked and assessed; (4) issues or barriers faced by liaison librarians and library departments in expanding or assessing liaison scholarly communication roles; and (5) future trends in scholarly communication relevant to liaison librarians. At the end of each interview, time was given for participants to provide additional details not covered in the set of questions. Notes were compiled and mined for themes and examples relating to the focus areas above.

To supplement the interviews, the current literature was surveyed for examples of liaison librarian scholarly communication activities and for appropriate methods or existing frameworks for assessing scholarly communication initiatives in general. This process included reviewing liaison librarian checklists and statements of core responsibilities to see what roles and responsibilities related to scholarly communications were listed.

Results
Areas, Focus, and Trends in Scholarly Communication

During the interviews, four areas of focus emerged: data curation, open access, library-supported publishing models, and digital scholarship. Not surprisingly, fourteen of the sixteen participants led with an example related to data curation activities, either institutional repository and data management services, or data life cycle and access issues. Open access (OA) and recent legislation on accessibility of funded research were also a considered important new areas of focus at the institutional level, and developing services and partnerships in support of OA was reported to be a high priority at four of the institutions. Of course, more traditional scholarly communication areas, like author rights and copyright, were also included in their responses, but these were not mentioned by any of the interviewees in the context of institutional priorities.

Digital scholarship was reported as an important emerging area of scholarly communication. Overall, the participants preferred a broad understanding of the term *digital scholarship* to include digital humanities, professional websites, and online scholarly profiles, as well as research management and scholarly workflow. Both scholarly communication librarians and subject librarians considered these areas a priority and spoke about institutional and departmental efforts to build services and capacity in support of digital scholarship. Finally, library-supported publishing services and models were considered important trends by librarians at four of the institutions surveyed. These institutions are currently developing or looking to develop new publishing services and models that support OA publishing, multimodal digital projects, and preservation of such projects.

Liaison Librarian Roles

Examples and expectations of liaison librarian roles in scholarly communication were diverse. While many of the activities mentioned fit comfortably within existing liaison librarian modes (reference, instruction, collections), the context or emphasis of the activities varied greatly. There were, however, a number of reported or suggested activities that go beyond these traditional modes. This variety perhaps illustrates the importance of local initiatives and priorities for determining liaison activities, as well as highlights the unique skills and experiences of individual librarians. There was no identifiable division of activity types reported among the participants, either by discipline or by librarian position (scholarly communication librarian versus subject library head).

The majority of examples reported involved referrals and consulting. Liaisons often make referrals to other appropriate units or experts, and this was seen as an important part of liaison work and as something essential to an organization's scholarly communication program. Consultation around scholarly communication issues, another activity in which liaisons routinely engage, is an area where liaisons are increasingly expanding their roles. Participants reported that liaisons consult regularly with faculty and researchers on a variety of topics, from professional websites and faculty portfolios to author rights, digital publishing options, and data curation. Liaisons are often invited by library colleagues and other units within the library to consult on internal projects and initiatives, as well as to report back to the scholarly communication librarian on trends and approaches in their specific disciplines. In all of the interviews, subject expertise and knowledge of researcher needs were viewed as important components of any scholarly communication program.

Other activities mentioned include partnering with scholarly communication units to talk with departments about services and teaching workshops related to scholarly communication issues. Workshop examples ranged from sessions on citation management to digital humanities and data management. A few of the interviewees described liaisons that are venturing beyond the sharing and advocacy that define core liaison duties and becoming more dynamically engaged in scholarly communication activities. At several institutions, it was noted that liaisons were creating and managing sets of digital materials; at others, liaisons were managing their own digital projects, as well as those of faculty and researchers.

While many liaisons are adopting these practices, a number of the subject library heads commented that they would like to see more liaisons pursue a deeper understanding of the scholarly communication issues relevant to their disciplines and engage more with faculty on this front. Some also commented that liaison librarians should be adopting good scholarly communication practices for themselves and modeling these behaviors. Modeling proper behaviors not only sets a good example for researchers, but what the liaison learns from the process can serve faculty more effectively than a librarian with secondhand knowledge. Some "good practices" might be moving their own research and data into the institutional repository or creating an online professional portfolio of their work. In a particularly striking example, one subject library is developing a departmental digital project to facilitate liaison reskilling. The liaison librarians will each contribute to the project in a number of areas, while learning about creating and disseminating their shared research in a digital environment.

Looking at more recent liaison checklists and general liaison statements of responsibility, we see many of these same roles and activities listed as core competencies or examples of best practices.[11] Common themes include helping researchers with author rights, promoting awareness of open and alternative publishing models, working with faculty to produce library-hosted content, and referring researchers to appropriate persons or units.

In contrast to the variety and depth of activities that came out of the interviews and that we are beginning to see in liaison responsibility descriptions, the current published literature suggests activities primarily related to information literacy, consultation, and referrals. It is clear from the interviews that liaisons are beginning to engage in much more dynamic ways, although how widely this is being adopted is unclear. It is time libraries begin expanding their ideas about liaison participation in scholarly communication initiatives and recognize in the literature more broadly the expanded role that liaison librarians are adopting in the scholarly communication arena.

Current Assessment Strategies

The interviews uncovered only a few examples of methods for assessing the scholarly communication activities of liaison librarians. Data-driven measures were the most common methods mentioned, specifically those related to tracking numbers of consultations, referrals, contact hours, and other transactions related to scholarly communication. Since librarians are already collecting this type of data for reference and instruction activities, it's a natural choice and convenient to add activities from new engagement areas. Another oft-mentioned measure involves looking at the total number of disciplinary publications in a repository or tracking their increase over a period of time. While these measures are acceptable and can be a useful indicator of broader trends, there was concern regarding the insufficiency of these measures alone. Numbers such as these say little about the level of engagement or the impact of the liaison's activities.

In addition to the data-driven measures, more qualitative approaches were suggested as a next step to evaluating liaison participation levels and impact of activities. Outlining specific scholarly communications duties in liaison core competencies and creating checklists of activities were perceived as effective measures of baseline proficiencies. This approach can also provide a clear and simple way for supervisors to track progress toward specified goals. Anecdotal accounts or narratives providing context to activities and illustrating impact were also viewed as an effective method for evaluating individual liaison librarians. Narratives can be particularly useful for documenting activities in promotion and tenure materials or for recording scholarly communication initiatives within a department or an organization. One institution reported using a spectrum-based instrument for gauging levels of engagement and the acquisition of new skills and knowledge, specifically in areas related to digital scholarship. What is most striking about this approach is its willingness to prioritize increased participation in new forms of scholarship for all librarians within the department.

Issues and Challenges

A number of overarching issues and challenges surfaced throughout the interviews. The difficulty of measuring participation and impact in scholarly communication was the most prevalent. Librarians commented on the disparate nature of the many disciplinary interests, institutional contexts, and liaison backgrounds. There was also a keen awareness of the complexities of measuring relationships and understanding, the foundations of any good scholarly communication program or initiative. Conflicting priorities were another big issue, an especially important consideration for the subject library heads. Liaison librarians are already donning a multitude of "hats," so how then do they prioritize scholarly communication? Recognizing that scholarly communication is an increasingly important area for liaisons is great, but what do they let go? All of the respondents who oversee liaison librarians were wary of perceived pressures for liaisons to do even more.

The Future of Scholarly Communication and Emerging Roles for Liaison Librarians

Despite the challenges mentioned, the librarians interviewed were each inspired by the changing scholarly communication landscape and looking forward to embracing new opportunities for liaison librarians. Scholarly communication is becoming less a specialty that can be managed by one position and will likely become more integrated into all positions. In particular, the general move toward openness and collaboration in research and publishing was viewed as a significant opportunity for liaisons to partner with faculty and the larger library. The shift to the digital was also noted as an important development affecting liaison roles. With the virtual mountains of digital assets, from electronic journal articles and books to images and data sets, researchers need guidance more than ever on managing their digital archiving practices and workflow. Finally, it was suggested that liaison librarians are well situated to bring scholarly societies into discussions and initiatives. Liaisons are often involved with the scholarly societies of the disciplines they serve, networking with their peers at other institutions and serving on committees. These connections allow libraries to elevate local scholarly communication initiatives to the national stage and can facilitate institutional participation in national efforts. Liaison librarians, with their deep understanding of disciplinary practices and institutional knowledge, are regarded as having a unique position to support and develop tools, services, and infrastructure to meet these emerging user needs.

Assessment Strategies

Assessment can take many forms and be employed to achieve a variety of ends. For the purposes of this chapter, assessment is not viewed primarily through the lens of the performance dialogue, but rather as a tool to be employed for self-assessment, for environmental scanning to underpin strategic planning for liaison initiatives, and for documenting and articulating the impact of the individual on their user populations.

Quantitative Assessment

Quantitative assessment methods for liaison's scholarly communication work are essential in our data-driven profession. A quantitative approach can best be defined in this context generally: any type of assessment that uses numbers as the basis for making inferences about the activities under evaluation.[12]

The reasoning that underpins collecting metrics is multifold. Strengths include the factual documentation of activities, which is often a baseline for assessment. As scholarly communication goals are deeply and explicitly integrated into library organizations at all levels, expectations for basic proficiencies and skills will be formalized as they are written into job descriptions. Collecting data relevant to these requirements will allow the individual to bring foundational numbers to annual performance evaluations. Documenting activities provides an excellent jumping-off point to begin a dialog centered on communicating the individual's value. Secondly, quantitative assessment is often viewed as highly persuasive due to its factual nature. In an economic milieu that requires librarians to justify how their time is spent, it is imperative to record the frequency of activities in order to frame them appropriately for supervisors. Liaison librarians must work with supervisors to identify, prioritize, and implement measures for personal data collection.

The strengths of data gathering naturally dovetail with specific strategic opportunities for liaisons engaging in scholarly communication work. For example, quantitative methods may reveal a trend that anecdotal and qualitative assessments do not. A librarian recording basic information about the number of research consultations and presentations related to scholarly communication topics will likely confirm or uncover the unique needs of the disciplines and local users she serves. (For instance, a new humanities librarian tracking copyright questions from art history and studio arts departments will naturally learn a great deal about how these user groups reuse images in surprisingly divergent ways: art history students may primarily be concerned with reproducing a work in an educational fair use context, while studio arts students look to library image collections for inspiration—raw materials for reuse and remixing). This, in turn, will inform how they prioritize their efforts and balance their scholarly communication work commitments. Similarly, data collection can assist in identifying lacunae in scholarly communications expertise or unmet needs of user populations. Once these gaps are identified, addressing them will help a liaison librarian best serve the user populations.

Finally, quantitative data should be fully integrated within an appropriate umbrella assessment framework for the organization. This will result in a rich, standardized, longitudinal data set with multiple uses, rather than a silo of scholarly communication assessment information that sits apart from what are traditionally viewed as core liaison job responsibilities (reference, instruction, collection development).[13] For example, a member library using a local database to record reference and instruction work for an organization such as the Association of Research Libraries can integrate scholarly communication liaison work into the database as a new data point, allowing the data to be compared directly to core library work over time.

Generating data around scholarly communication liaison work also has shortcomings. One inherent weakness is that data without context are effectively "dumb." Without the appropriate interpretative lens to give the data weight and meaning, metrics may have little value to anyone beyond the practitioner librarian and her intuitive understanding of the accomplishments the data represent. The limitation of context lends itself to another concern: data misuse. In an environment where supervisors or administrators may not understand or value the scholarly communication needs being met by disciplinary liaisons, librarians must proactively communicate how their prioritized work is supporting the mission of the departments to which they liaise (in addition to the library itself). Other weaknesses of quantitative assessment include concerns about data quality (underreported or inconsistently entered data) and the return on investment of librarians' time as they document their work.

It is essential for liaison librarians to identify and prioritize measures for personal data collection. Specific data points will vary between individuals based on disciplinary and institutional needs and the practitioner librarian's personal aptitudes and inclinations. A baseline might include the following mainstream, service-related behaviors on the topic of scholarly communication:

- number of formal consultations and substantial informal discussions

- number of referrals to individuals or organizations with scholarly communication expertise
- number of presentations or publications related to scholarly communication topics
- number of blog postings, tweets, or other social or alternative media outlets

As data on specific points become increasingly important, liaison librarians can move beyond tracking simply the number of transactions to more meaningful measures. For example, a librarian who finds that much of her one-on-one consultation time with graduate students is spent explaining author rights and disciplinary requirements for publishing could begin recording student contact hours. The contact hours data in aggregate could then be used to convey the need for greater disciplinary coaching on these issues.

Provision of increasingly sophisticated scholarly communication services and resources will likely require specialized measures. One might assess outreach efforts to faculty by the number or percentage of individuals reached, or by an attempt to quantify the impact of the liaison's efforts on faculty behavior. (One possible example: counting the number of faculty publications deposited in an institutional repository after a concerted effort on the librarian's part—regardless of strategy employed—to encourage voluntary submissions.) Specialized measures are often more time-intensive to develop and employ and, as such, should be employed purposefully to yield an insightful, useful data set. Over time, specialized quantitative measures that have widespread utility and value will become established alongside the core data libraries already collect.

Qualitative Assessment

Qualitative assessment can "encompass a variety of methodologies, including observation, interviewing, [and] document analysis."[14] It may be employed in concert with quantitative methods, or in place of them when a numeric approach would prove unmanageable or uninformative.

Qualitative methods of assessment allow practitioner subject liaison librarians to convey a vivid and personalized narrative centered on their achievements. This approach allows assessors to "make sense" of what they are attempting to evaluate—in effect, learning as they construct an evaluative framework to flesh out. The reflective nature of many qualitative assessment methods allows for insights, self-awareness, and personal progress when assessing scholarly communication work. Therefore, qualitative assessment is uniquely suited to liaison librarians expanding their personal competencies.

One foundational qualitative method for assessing liaison scholarly communication work is to create a personal inventory of activities. Essentially, the practitioner can generate lists of what she has been doing, would like to do, and has not yet had the opportunity to do. This is a good first step for librarians new to documenting, organizing, and reporting out their work. In the professional literature, such lists are well established. Librarians can look to the ACRL Scholarly Communications Toolkit, local liaison librarian checklists (if they exist), and open resources such as University of Minnesota's concise, readable scholarly communication "Core Competencies for Liaison Librarians."[15] Enterprising librarians can reverse-engineer their institutional definition of scholarly communication, parsing it to find broad overarching areas in which to file their own inventory and disciplinary work. Ideally, librarian-generated lists can be cross-referenced with supervisor, department, library-wide, and disciplinary scholarly communication priorities. In time, it is realistic to expect that subject specialist librarians will begin to customize and generate their own discipline-specific inventories. This will allow subject librarians to benchmark against their peers at other institutions, something that may be more immediately useful than comparisons to their colleagues working with different disciplines. This final step will allow individuals to further align their efforts to the priorities of the many groups to which they report. Dovetailing individual assessment with a broader framework is imperative; where a broader framework doesn't exist, individual assessment can provide grassroots, crowd-sourced content for an overarching plan.

A second method of assessment, gleaned from library instruction literature, is writing a prose personal reflection. As self-assessment, a personal meditation could be free-form. Guiding questions can be used to provide structure and direction should such an essay be incorporated into a work plan, annual review, or materials for promotion. A standardized, department or library-wide prompt could be used for institution-wide assessment. However, such a prompt would have to be carefully constructed and presented to librarians for the goal of the standardization to be made explicit and relevant to all. A broad prompt could appear irrelevant should it not take into consideration the liaison librarians' focus on activities germane to their discipline and users.

Another method of qualitative assessment borrowed from instructional design is to employ a rubric or gap analysis. The distinction between these two tools is an important one: a rubric is a performance evaluation tool, while a gap analysis is a planning tool. A sample rubric developed expressly for this chapter appears in appendix A, Scholarly Communication Activities Evaluation Rubric for Librarians, and can be customized to individual needs. The benefits of rubrics are multifold, as they clearly delineate what is required of an individual. When properly constructed, a rubric makes evaluation quick and easy, as it provides a clear framework for assessing and weighing the import of multiple factors—judgments that would appear wholly subjective when evaluated without structure. Rubrics are not appropriate for situations in which the elements being evaluated are not clearly and simply delineated. Instead, using a rubric suggests a high level of planning has resulted in this document, with its explicit wording. Liaisons not yet ready to employ or create their own rubric can begin by using a gap analysis. A gap analysis can be constructed by developing a list of aptitudes and using a simple Likert scale to rank the individuals' proficiency, expressing how much work an individual needs employ to reach her goal. Ideally, elements for a gap analysis would have been identified by other methods of assessment.

Qualitative assessment methods are widely accepted in libraries, although the validity and reliability of the information collected is inherently harder to establish. For this reason, any assessment beyond personal use should likely employ both qualitative and quantitative methods to convey the fullest and most persuasive record of the liaison librarian's achievements.

A Framework for Scholarly Communication Activities

To more effectively use qualitative measures such as those mentioned above, a framework is often needed to give context and points of comparison to the liaison's activities. A framework can help to ensure that assessment is more uniform while simultaneously allowing for flexibility and customization. Here, a framework is proposed that reflects the range of activities in which liaisons participate and encourages a variety of levels of engagement so that librarians can play to their strengths and disciplinary needs.

The framework is built on a set of spheres of activities, or *modalities*, around which to frame and structure self- or supervisor-assisted evaluation. With these modalities, the authors attempt to capture and classify the continuum of activities in which liaisons participate: exploration, engagement, advocacy, agency, and innovation (figure 6.1). Each modality can be assessed on its own or in concert with one or more of the other modalities for a holistic assessment of an individual's, department's, or organization's contributions to scholarly communication initiatives. While some modalities will inherently have higher impact than others, one need not consider them hierarchical. Depending on context, advocacy or agency may be of higher value than innovation, or engagement might be what is most appropriate. For each modality, possible goals and select examples of activities are listed to help define the category.

Figure 6.1

Framework of a Liaison Librarian's Scholarly Communication Activities

Exploration

- **Focus:** pursuing personal development and seeking to better understand current issues and trends in scholarly communication
- **Goals and activities:** understanding local needs and initiatives, investigating the literature, taking advantage of training opportunities, and identifying aptitudes and interests relating to scholarly communication
- **Note:** While the impact of exploration may not be as apparent as those of other modalities, we must recognize its role in the development of scholarly communication initiatives. The information gathered might inspire or impact future projects and activities, as well as contribute to ongoing scholarly communication measures that rely on an informed cadre of librarians. This modality is essential at all levels of engagement: from beginners acquainting themselves with issues in their disciplines to expert librarian wanting to keep up with the changing landscape or cutting-edge initiatives.

Engagement

- **Focus:** putting knowledge into practice by relating it to other aspects of one's job and sharing with a wider audience
- **Goals and activities:** translating scholarly communication concepts and practices to stakeholders in academic disciplines,

applying expertise to core liaison roles such as research support and collection development, modeling good scholarly communication behaviors, and participating in communities of practice

- **Note:** This modality mirrors closely the day-to-day activities in which liaisons already engage, although with content that is perhaps unfamiliar. It should be quite easy for interested librarians to contribute to scholarly communication in this way. Communities of practice can make adopting this new area even easier by offering a supportive network in which to solve problems, share information, reuse assets, document practices, and map collective knowledge.[16] The ACRL Scholarly Communication Toolkit and the Minnesota Liaison Toolkit, mentioned above, are good examples of communities of practice to this end.

Advocacy

- **Focus:** defining and articulating values, agendas, and approaches around scholarly communication issues and engaging in substantive dialogue
- **Goals and activities:** championing certain values or community needs in consortial or national efforts or through dialog in public forums and media, considering local issues in a broader context, contributing to standards, and participating actively in communities and initiatives

Agency

- **Focus:** effecting change, stewarding agendas and initiatives, forming more formal collaborations, and taking on leadership roles

- **Goals and activities:** implementing tools or infrastructures in support of scholarly communication activities, systematizing or establishing more formal frameworks for services and practices, prioritizing goals and activities, and leading or collaborating on projects and initiatives
- **Note:** Fewer liaisons will have the time or resources to realize this type of activity, but should nevertheless be encouraged if they have the interest and expertise. Many librarians and institutions are modifying the roles of librarians to reflect a more dynamic, collaborative service model, and with the changes taking place in reference and collection development (more consultative, less desk time; large packages and approval plans over firm orders), librarians may be able to let go, at least in part, of some of the more traditional roles in favor of new ones such as these.

Innovation

- **Focus:** developing new concepts or tools to meet community needs or applying these in novel ways
- **Goals and activities:** exercising leadership and expertise in new and emerging areas, using knowledge of top-level trends and insights for national or industry-level decision-making planning, and supporting or participating in research and development activities

Implications and Future Research

While this exploratory study suggests that liaison librarians do not yet actively document their scholarly communication activities, it is clear that liaisons are participating and welcome real opportunities to expand their scholarly communication roles. Employing diverse assessment measures is an opportunity for liaison librarians to both define and expand their roles and evaluate appropriate levels of participation to best serve their user community. Furthermore, the approaches and framework presented might serve as a useful method for assessing the more traditional roles and responsibilities related to reference, instruction, and collection development. Liaisons actively participate outside their disciplinary boundaries and in the national arena more than ever and are contributing in more dynamic ways. Since this framework attempts to reframe the modes in which liaisons already perform, taking into account the changing and diverse roles of liaisons, it could provide a new model for approaching liaison assessment, prioritization, and goal setting in areas beyond scholarly communication.

Still, further study is needed to expand on the literature and resources that can aid the liaison librarian in defining her role and provide good models of scholarly communication activities. Insights gleaned from practice will come with increased scrutiny and reflection, leading directly to the crystallization of research questions. One logical extension of the exploratory study conducted for this chapter would be to expand the sample size to ensure greater diversity of opinion. Another option is to refocus on a specific subset of subject specialist liaison librarians in an effort to come to a deep, fundamental understanding of that discipline. This approach to future study should be undertaken with the goal not only of expanding understanding, but also of identifying transferable or universal insights. Finally, an emphasis on evaluating the individual implies that the parts of a larger whole have been touched on, but not fully explored. Discovering how assessment of the individual interconnects with and, ideally, enhances other types of assessment should be a priority. Starting points for convergence include evaluations of library scholarly communication programs (be they departmental or the result of a decentralized, coordinated effort) and social science studies of scholars' attitudes and behaviors toward scholarly communication.

Showing librarians "how to" is the first step to increased liaison engagement. Coupled with individual assessment, this practical training can serve as a strong foundation for a liaison librarian program that values and responds to institutional context while advancing the goals of the library and profession. One continuing challenge is the need to create real, meaningful opportunities for liaisons to participate in scholarly communication efforts within their home institution. The assessment methods proposed in this chapter will hopefully assist in identifying, pursuing, and sharing those opportunities, while at the same time spurring self-starters to generate and advocate for involvement on a grassroots level.

Notes

1. *Research Library Issues* no. 265, Special Issue on Liaison Librarian Roles (August 2009), http://publications.arl.org/rli265.

2. Joy Kirchner, "Scholarly Communications: Planning for the Integration of Liaison Librarian Roles," in *Research Library Issues* no. 265: 22–28.

3. Kara Whatley, "New Roles of Liaison Librarians: A Liaison's Perspective," in *Research Library Issues* no. 265: 29–32.

4. Mary Auckland, *Re-skilling for Research: An Investigation into the Role and Skills of Subject and Liaison Librarians Required to Effectively Support the Evolving Information Needs of Researchers* (London: Research Libraries UK, January 2012), www.voced.edu.au/content/ngv50773.

5. Ibid., 63.

6. Stephanie Davis-Kahl and Merinda Kaye Hensley, eds., *Common Ground at the Nexus of Information Literacy and Scholarly Communication* (Chicago: Association of College and Research Libraries, 2013), http://digitalcommons.iwu.edu/bookshelf/36.

7. Working Group on Intersections of Scholarly Communication and Information Literacy, *Intersections of Scholarly Communication and Information Literacy: Creating Strategic Collaborations for a Changing Academic Environment* (Chicago: Association of College and Research Libraries, 2013), http://acrl.ala.org/intersections.

8. Ibid., 20.

9. Tracy Gabridge, "The Last Mile: Liaison Roles in Curating Science and Engineering Research Data," in *Research Library Issues* no. 265: 15.

10. Mark P. Newton, Christopher C. Miller, and Marianne Stowell Bracke, "Librarian Roles in Institutional Repository Data Set Collecting: Outcomes of a Research Library Task Force," *Collection Management* 36, no. 1 (2010): 22.

11. Two recent in-house documents on librarian responsibilities: Ohio State University Libraries, "A Framework for the Engaged Librarian: Building on Our Strengths," last modified October 22, 2012, https://carmenwiki.osu.edu/download/attachments/37010332/Engaged+Librarian+Document.pdf?version=1&modificat

ionDate=1362663472574; Task Force on Subject Librarian Re-Visioning, *Engaging with Library Users: Sharpening Our Vision as Subject Librarians* (Durham, NC: Duke University Libraries, 2011), http://library.duke.edu/sites/default/files/dul/about/subject-librarian-report-2011.pdf

12. Adapted from *International Encyclopedia of the Social Sciences*, 2nd ed., ed. William A. Darity Jr., (Detroit: Macmillan Reference, 2008), s.v. "Methods, Quantitative."

13. Adapted from Stephen Pinfield, "The Changing Role of Subject Librarians in Academic Libraries," *Journal of Librarianship and Information Science* 33, no. 1 (2001): 32–38.

14. Adapted from *International Encyclopedia of the Social Sciences*, s.v. "Methods, Qualitative."

15. *Scholarly Communication Toolkit* home page, Association of College and Research Libraries, accessed 10/30/2013. http://scholcomm.acrl.ala.org; "Core Competencies for Liaison Librarians," University of Minnesota Libraries, last modified June 11, 2012, https://wiki.lib.umn.edu/ScholarlyCommunication/Core-competencies.html.

16. Adapted from Etienne Wenger, "Communities of Practice: A Brief Introduction," June 2006, http://wenger-trayner.com/wp-content/uploads/2012/01/06-Brief-introduction-to-communities-of-practice.pdf.

Appendix 6
Scholarly Communication Activities Evaluation Rubric for Liaison Librarians

This rubric was developed to help liaison librarians assess scholarly communication activities and as a precursor to managing personal projects. It can also be used to perform an environmental scan at the department or institutional level to gain a better understanding of current scholarly communication support practices. Liaisons are invited to customize this rubric to their needs. To download the rubric, visit: https://scholarsphere.psu.edu/files/pv63g1444

1. Select or develop your own target area.
2. Reflect on your level of sophistication for each modality, creating a list of achievements on a separate piece of paper.
3. Transfer your achievements to the rubric, using specific examples.
4. Determine where the gaps lie. Have you taken for granted specific "beginning" or "developing" steps that have lead to "mastery"?
5. Identify what modalities or levels of mastery you would like to advance. What might achievements on each level look like? What are the next steps?

Target Area: ☐ Open Access / Author Rights ☐ Data Management ☐ Digital Scholarship ☐ Other _____

Modality	Beginning	Developing	Mastering
Exploration	• I have identified resources to further my understanding on the topic	• I have an understanding of the broad outlines of the topic or issue • I have identified specific issues or topics for further exploration	• I am well versed in specific issues • I feel comfortable sharing what I've learned with others
Engagement	• I share my knowledge with others in broader contexts • I make appropriate referrals	• I share my knowledge in the form of workshops, forums, and guides • I participate in conversations around the issues	• I contribute to the community of practice by sharing resources that I've created for reuse by the community • I effectively consult with researchers
Advocacy	• I have identified a cause or issue for which I would like to advocate	• I have researched the cause or issue and understand what is at stake/identified key stakeholders • I can articulate my values and agenda related to this issue or cause	• I actively engage in substantive dialog to raise awareness of the issue or cause • I actively participate in setting standards and building community and initiatives in support of the cause or issue
Agency	• I have identified a problem and begun to research and identify possible solutions • I can outline specific objectives and outcomes to address the problem	• I have evaluated and tested a possible solution • I have consulted with experts or others working on this problem	• I have implemented appropriate solutions • I have shared outcomes/strategies with the larger community
Innovation	• I have identified a problem for which I have found no appropriate existing solution	• I have articulated and developed potential solutions • I have balanced and evaluated risks and outcomes	• I have tested and refined iterations of the solution • I have shared the innovation to extend the solution to broader communities, inviting feedback and customization

Chapter Seven

The Library as Platform

Assessing Outreach and Engagement in the Library of the Future

Marcy Bidney

Curator
American Geographical Society Library
University of Wisconsin–Milwaukee
Milwaukee, WI

Introduction

There has long been an identity crisis in libraries, fear permeating the field that we are no longer relevant, our constituents often saying they can find what they need on the Internet without the help of a librarian. As a result, we continually try to come up with ways to bring people back into the library, admittedly with mixed results. Technological advances ensure that we find ourselves in a continued state of change. Instruction, reference, collection development, and outreach to our communities have all changed, and technology has been the crux of most of these changes. As a result, many libraries are in the process of transforming themselves from places where people search for and find information, check out books, and obtain traditional reference services to a place where people consume, produce, and curate information and collaborate using the many resources in the library—both information resources and technological resources. These libraries are in the process of reinventing themselves, moving from the role of traditional gatekeepers of information to the role of facilitators for those who want to use information and technology in creative and innovative ways for the enhancement of research and learning.

Technological advances are also changing how we look at, organize, and talk about library collections. Librarians are able to virtually organize digital materials in ways that are inherently different from the ways print materials are organized. The development of digital collections within libraries has enhanced the ability to bring similar collections together, both internally and externally, creating a new "special collection," possibly curated for a particular audience within the community or as collaboration with a local cultural heritage institution with collections that complement the library's. These newly developed "special collections" differ from traditional special collections in that they are not necessarily rare items found in a special department of the library. They are merely collections of items in the general collections of a library, possibly complemented by collections of items at local cultural heritage institutions, that are unique, to either the local area, the state, or the region. These changes have also provided an avenue for libraries to work with organizations outside of campus, including museums, historical societies, etc., and it is with the development and discovery of these new "special collections" that there are new opportunities for academic libraries to engage with their communities.

Additionally, if, as Hugh Rundle states, libraries need to become "a platform for enabling innovation, learning, and cultural development to occur in our communities,"[1] then this latest round of change leaves libraries having to reassess the avenues and methods they use for outreach and engagement. Libraries need to engage with, not just reach out to, local, regional, and state cultural institutions in their communities to bring users in, to facilitate knowledge creation and learning, and to help users understand and take advantage of innovative ways of engaging with library collections. On campus, student engagement and outreach is still a vital role for libraries to maintain, but for new, future-focused service models to be successful, outreach and engagement need to include a focus on campus grant coordination offices, formal and informal interdisciplinary research institutes, and collaboration with faculty in the development and enhancement of digital scholarship.

Outreach and engagement activities permeate all aspects of librarianship and are not limited to librarians with those words in their titles. Subject librarians, liaison librarians, special collection librarians or curators, reference librarians, and instruction librarians all have the responsibility to perform outreach and engagement activities. The issue of assessment of outreach and engagement activities is a crucial one that academic libraries need to be discussing because, as mentioned above, the role of libraries and the activities that occur within their walls are changing dramatically and librarians need to have a better understanding of what is working and what is not during this important time. Additionally, librarians need to provide concrete examples of their work for the purposes of retention, promotion, or tenure, and one of the easiest ways to do this is to have a holistic, individual assessment program in place. This chapter will focus on providing guidance and tools to use for individual assessment of liaison librarian efforts in outreach and engagement and will provide examples of how librarians can document the impact of new programs and services.

Defining Outreach and Engagement

Examining the definitions of *outreach* and *engagement* is necessary to ensure that the reader understands the difference between the two when talking about the assessment of liaison activities. *Outreach* and *engagement* are often used interchangeably when actually they describe two different, but similar, activities.

Outreach

Merriam-Webster defines outreach as "the extending of services or assistance beyond current or usual limits."[2] Harris and Weller, in their 2012 article about outreach and special collections in libraries, define outreach as "the proactive endeavors by special collections staff to increase awareness and use of their collections and the professional mission of special collections librarians and archivists, both within and outside the academy."[3] In an effort to try to better define outreach for special collection librarians and archivists, Tamar Chute conducted a survey, asking 234 archivists a series of questions intended to determine how they view outreach versus basic services. Chute's conclusion resulted in the following definition of outreach: "*any* activity of an archive or manuscript repository intended to *educate* potential *and current* users about their holdings, *services, and institutional history* as well as their research and reference values. *Examples include: exhibits, presentations, reference, and donor relations.*"[4]

Tina Schneider offers a slightly different, more forward-looking definition of outreach in her article "Outreach: Why, How and Who? Academic Libraries and Their Involvement in the Community." She specifically states that outreach focuses "less on circulation policies and shared libraries, and more on independent efforts of libraries to move beyond their walls or traditional clientele to interact with their surrounding community."[5]

The one thing that all of these definitions have in common is that they involve raising users' awareness of library services. The act of reaching out by librarians is typically not seen as a mutually beneficial relationship. This idea is reflected in the literature, which discusses plenty of examples of outreach services for traditional users to make them more aware of basic library services and collections. In these examples, the users are the focus and benefit from learning more about, and potentially using, library services they were previously unaware of. The examples include the development of special webpages, exhibits, presentations, workshops, etc. In these examples, the library does not necessarily benefit from the efforts, though librarians hope that use of services and collections would increase due to the outreach efforts.

Engagement

In 1999, the Kellogg Commission on the Future of State and Land-Grant Universities issued its third report, titled *Returning to Our Roots: The Engaged Institution.*[6] This report was a response to growing public frustration with higher education that was seen as out of date. The Kellogg Commission concluded that "it is time to go beyond outreach and service to what the Kellogg Commission now defines as 'engagement.'"[7] The report defined engaged institutions as "institutions that have redesigned their teaching, research, and extension and service functions to become even more sympathetically and productively involved with their community, however community may be defined."[8] This report really was the beginning of the wave of change that brought engagement into the forefront of university and thus academic library missions. The response from universities varied. Some, such as Ohio State University, Michigan State University and Auburn University embraced this new ideal and have been leaders in the implementation of engagement throughout all aspects of their universities.

In libraries, engagement can mean a number of different things, depending on the type of library and librarian, collections, and resources of the library and staffing. The authors of ARL's *SPEC Kit 312* back up the one-way street view of outreach programs by saying "outreach programs on campus have typically focused on the provision of access to services and resources to members of the community."[9] Future-focused libraries should include more engagement with users in their outreach and marketing efforts. How is engagement different from traditional outreach? "While the concept of engagement is still emerging and is not uniformly understood, it is typically distinguished from earlier understandings of 'outreach' by its focus on collaboration between campus and community to address common concerns and the mutual benefit that accrues to partners on both sides as the result of engagement activities."[10]

In the survey, authors of the ARL SPEC Kit define engagement as "programs demonstrating a library and/or institutional commitment to community partnerships, service to professional communities outside their primary user groups and to teaching, research, and extension and service functions"[11]

Where the library-user outreach relationship is a one-way relationship, the library-user engagement relationship is mutually beneficial: the library or librarian gains as much as the user who is being engaged. The primary focus of engagement is to bring the expertise of librarians to users beyond the campus community. The librarian benefits by gaining experience in action research, and the users gain a better understanding of the issue at hand. "Engagement goes well beyond extension, conventional outreach, and even most conceptions of public service."[12] If academic libraries are moving toward becoming a platform or lab where learning, innovation, and cultural development occur and where an expanding definition for special collections is reality, then user engagement, instead of simply outreach, is where efforts for thoughtfully and carefully planned engagement should be focused. Understanding these differences is important for the development of individual and programmatic assessment activities because the assessment of outreach will be very different from the assessment of engagement and the ability to show success in each these areas of activity will be increasingly important for librarians.

Individual Assessment of Outreach and Engagement Liaison Librarian Activities

The literature on outreach and engagement efforts of all types of libraries provides some examples of assessment of programs and services. Where the literature falls short is in providing examples for librarians who wish to perform individual assessment for promotion, tenure, and retention purposes. Assessment is an important activity that needs to be performed for librarians to modify programs, demonstrate positive outcomes, and justify continuing or additional support, financially or otherwise, in a constantly competitive budget environment. This is a process that deserves better coverage in the literature.

This section will pull from three main sources to examine how program assessments and self-assessments for organizations or universities can be applied to developing an individual assessment tool for librarians who are assigned outreach duties. These three sources are Auburn University's Faculty Handbook, the Committee for Institutional Cooperation's (CIC) Committee on Engagement's categories of engagement, and the National Review Board for the Scholarship of Engagement's criteria for the assessment of the scholarship of engagement. These sources were chosen because they are focused on outreach and engagement in higher education and would most likely be criteria that academic librarians would be familiar with and be expected to follow. All have common elements that make adaptation easy.

Auburn University's Faculty Handbook has an entire section on outreach focused on the intent and outcomes of outreach and aimed at aiding faculty in documenting and assessing their outreach efforts for retention, promotion, and tenure. The policy lists six conditions that need to be met in order for the activity to be considered outreach. These six conditions can easily be applied when planning and assessing outreach and engagement efforts of librarians. According to the Auburn policy, outreach efforts must have:

- "a substantive link with significant human needs and societal problems, issues or concerns"
- "a direct application of knowledge to significant human needs and societal problems, issues or concerns"
- a "utilization of the faculty member's academic and professional expertise"
- an ultimate purpose that "is for the public or common good"
- generation of "new knowledge … for the discipline and/or the audience or clientele"
- "a clear link/relationship between the program/activities and an appropriate academic unit's mission"[13]

While not an explicit set of criteria for evaluation of outreach and engagement, these criteria can be used in the development of a matrix or rubric for individual and programmatic assessment. The Auburn criteria are broad and general enough to be applied to librarians, and in fact, the librarians at Auburn have faculty status and so would be expected to follow these criteria when developing and evaluating outreach and engagement programs.

The Committee on Institutional Cooperation (CIC) is made up of the Big Ten universities plus the University of Chicago. These institutions work together and share resources to advance missions and serve the common good, using faculty expertise and the development of innovative programs. Within the CIC, there are a number of committees and groups that meet regularly and work collaboratively on projects. The CIC Committee on Engagement works to promote engagement at member universities and in 2005 drafted a resource guide for engaged scholarship. The guide offers the following seven categories of indicators that institutions can use for documenting scholarly engagement:

1. Evidence of Institutional Commitment to Engagement
2. Evidence of Institutional Resource Commitments to Engagement
3. Evidence that Students are Involved in Engagement and Outreach Activities
4. Evidence that Faculty and Staff are Engaged with External Constituents
5. Evidence that Institutions are Engaged with their Communities
6. Evidence of Assessing the Impact and Outcomes of Engagement
7. Evidence of Resource/Revenue Opportunities Generated through Engagement[14]

These criteria more directly address the evaluation of outreach and engagement activities. The full resource guide provides subcategories under these headings that can be used for more detailed development of outcomes and benchmarks.

The criteria below, set by the National Review Board (NRB) for the Scholarship of Engagement, while extremely useful for setting up a comprehensive individual assessment model, can also be used for peer-review committees and others involved in the evaluation of a librarian's contribution to the scholarship of engagement. The list of criteria from the NRB is lengthy, and for the sake of brevity, only those criteria most relevant to library work, namely goals, results, communication, and critique, are discussed here. The entire list of criteria can be found at the National Review Board for the Scholarship of Engagement's website. The NRB's criteria are as follows:

Goals/Questions
- Does the scholar state the basic purpose of the work and its value for the public good?
- Is there an "academic fit" with the scholar's role, departmental and university mission?
- Does the scholar define objectives that are realistic and achievable?

Results
- Does the scholar achieve the goals?
- Does the scholar's work add consequentially to the discipline and to the community?
- Does the scholar's work open additional areas for further exploration and collaboration?

Communication/Dissemination
- Does the scholar communicate/disseminate to appropriate academic and public audiences consistent with the mission of the institution?

- Does the scholar use appropriate forums for communicating work to the intended audience?
- Does the scholar present information with clarity and integrity?

Reflective Critique
- What are the sources of evidence informing the critique?
- In what way has the community perspective informed the critique?
- Does the scholar use evaluation to learn from the work and to direct future work?[15]

Since these criteria are also developed specifically for evaluation of the scholarship of outreach and engagement, they provide another resource for librarians seeking to develop a systematic approach to individual or programmatic assessment.

These three sets of criteria can be blended to develop a comprehensive, ongoing program of individual and programmatic assessment for outreach and engagement in academic libraries. When talking about developing a method for assessment of liaison activities in outreach and engagement, librarians should have a variety of tools in their toolbox from which to choose. In addition to criteria similar to those listed above, librarians should have a clear understanding of the library's and the university's strategic plans, missions, and vision. It is important to articulate attainable goals and a clear course of action for engagement. Librarians should develop this plan with their supervisor or mentor and preferably with the constituency with whom the engagement will take place. In goal setting for individual assessment three factors are crucial:

1. Identifying priority groups and programs, both internal (in the library) and external (in the community).

2. Situating these priorities within the context of both the missions and the strategic plans of the library and the university.

3. Ensuring that goals are not developed in a vacuum and involve the group or organization the librarian plans to reach out to or engage with for successful service development. All care should also be taken to ensure that the goals set are attainable for all parties involved.

Librarians should also keep in mind that "successful outreach programs are more than public relations or promotional activities. In fact, they are generally based upon the basic principles of marketing and rely heavily on planning and management theory"[16] and should look to these theories, in conjunction with the information presented here, for guidance in the development of planning materials.

In outreach and engagement, it is important to incorporate a mixture of formal and informal assessment methods along with a mixture of quantitative and qualitative measures in order to capture the whole picture of the activities being assessed. The importance of outreach and engagement work is difficult to reflect in statistical measures alone. The assessment therefore benefits from the addition of qualitative descriptions that highlight the work and its importance to the library, university, and community. This combination of efforts also allows librarians to assess fledgling, innovative programs, which may not have generated enough quantitative data to be properly analyzed.

Developing an Outreach and Engagement Individual Assessment Matrix

With all of this information, a librarian should be able to create a custom assessment matrix to use for individual and programmatic evaluation. Table 7.1 is a basic framework developed with different parts of the criteria from sources mentioned earlier. This framework focuses on the two main areas that librarians would be concerned with in conducting an individual assessment of their outreach and engagement liaison activities—their duties as a librarian, called Librarianship, and their duties as a scholar, called Scholarship. This matrix is by no means comprehensive and should be taken and adapted to each individual librarian and possibly each project or overall program of outreach and engagement.

Typically benchmarking is an effective method for evaluation of activities. But benchmarking is a difficult activity to perform in this case since outreach and engagement liaison activities at libraries and universities will be different enough to prevent any real comparison from occurring. Even peer-comparison benchmarks should be avoided due to the different nature of outreach and engagement between liaison librarians in the same library.

The questions asked as indicators should vary based on a number of factors, including the size of the university and its library, the amount of resources available, the amount of time a liaison librarian devotes to outreach and engagement activities, and the desired outcomes of those activities. The matrix could be applied to something as simple as developing a social media strategy and be used to gauge its success and impact on the two main categories of Librarianship and Scholarship. It could also be applied to a large-scale library development program aimed at engaging donors and friends of the library groups. The adaptation possibilities are numerous and require just time and energy for development.

Conclusion

Assessing outreach and engagement can be a daunting and somewhat difficult task due to the amorphous quality of these activities. When approaching the assessment of a new outreach or engagement activity, it is always best to start small. Choose one or two simple aspects of the activity on which to solicit feedback and gather statistics; use some of the examples in table 7.1 to develop a small assessment tool, and administer that tool as effectively as possible. Once you feel comfortable with the

Table 7.1
Individual and Programmatic Assessment Matrix for Outreach and Engagement

Element		Example Questions and Indicators
Librarianship	Formal/ Qualitative	• How many meetings with users were held? • What resources were used for promotion of the program/project? • How many users were reached? • How many individuals were involved both at the library and in the community? • How many additional partnerships, both on and off campus, if any, resulted from this program/project? • Surveys • Social networking statistics • Digital collection use statistics • Length of time of the program (How many months, years, etc. did it last?) • Is there an assessment mechanism in place to ensure the program does not go stagnant?
	Informal/ Quantitative	• Describe how the program/project fits into the library's or university's mission and strategic plan. • Describe how stakeholders participated in the program/project from beginning to end. • Describe, or provide examples of, any documents developed for or during the program/project. • Were project goals met? • Were results valued by users involved? • Was access to library resources (print and/or digital) increased? • Was access to community resources increased? • How did this program/project benefit the library? • How did this program/project benefit the users/community? • Describe the impacts of the program/project on all involved. • How can this program/project be used as a model for other libraries/communities? • Were there any changes in policies, collections, etc. as a result of this program/project? • Does the program/project fit well with the skills and knowledge of the librarian?
Scholarship	Formal/ Qualitative	• Survey users for their feedback about the program/project. • Gather statistics from available sources about the program/project. • Was a research paper or presentation generated from the program/project? If so, how many times has it been cited?
	Informal/ Quantitative	• Were new and innovative ideas used for program/project development? • Did any new or innovative ideas come up as a result of the program/project? • How well was the program/project defined and developed? What would be different next time? • Is the plan for the program/project sustainable? • Are the users involved with generation of new knowledge and expertise? • Was there any informal feedback received about the program/project?

development and deployment of these smaller assessment activities, they can be expanded to be more inclusive of each outreach and engagement activity performed. The most important aspect is to just start someplace, become comfortable with the activity, and develop tools that best tell the story of the activities you perform and their impact on the library and community at large.

Many librarians will need the tools to assess engagement and outreach in their assessment toolbox. The changing nature of libraries and librarianship demands that we continuously seek new avenues for outreach and engagement. In order to determine which avenues are successful and for which we need increased funding and advocacy, librarians need to be able to provide concrete proof of success. In a climate of declining budgets, staffing, and support in libraries, it is very important that we continue to take the time and effort to show our value not only to our supervisors, peers, campus users, and partners, but also to users and partners off campus as well. Libraries and librarians need to continuously take stock of their liaison activities and how well those activities fit within the framework of the future directions of their institutions, of the disciplines they are responsible for, and of the future directions of libraries and librarianship. Developing a comprehensive individual assessment program is an effective means of providing this information, especially over a long period of time as successes build.

Notes

1.   Hugh Rundle, "Libraries as Software: Dematerializing, Platforms and Returning to First Principles, *It's Not About the Books* (blog), April 4, 2012, www.hughrundle.net/2012/04/04/libraries-as-software-dematerialising-platforms-and-returning-to-first-principles.

2.   *Merriam-Webster's Collegiate Dictionary*, 11th ed., s.v. "outreach."

3.   Valerie A. Harris and Ann C. Weller, "Use of Special Collections as an Opportunity for Outreach in the Academic Library," *Journal of Library Administration* 52, no. 3–4 (2012): 294–303, doi:10.1080/01930826.2012.684508.

4. Tamar G. Chute, "What's in a Name? Outreach vs. Basic Services: A Survey of College and University Archivists," *Journal of Archival Organization* 1, no. 2 (2002): 21, doi:10.1300/J201v01n02_02.

5. Tina Schneider, "Outreach: Why, How and Who? Academic Libraries and Their Involvement in the Community," *Reference Librarian* 39, no. 82 (2003): 200, doi:10.1300/J120v39n82_13.

6. Kellogg Commission on the Future of State and Land-Grant Universities, *Returning to Our Roots: The Engaged Institution*, 3rd report (Washington, DC: National Association of State Universities and Land-Grant Colleges, 1999).

7. Ibid., 9.

8. Ibid.

9. Scott Walter and Lori Goetsch, *Public Engagement: SPEC Kit 312* (Washington, DC: Association of Research Libraries, 2009), 11.

10. Ibid,

11. Ibid., 18.

12. Kellogg Commission on the Future of State and Land-Grant Universities, *Returning to Our Roots: The Engaged Institution*, 3rd report (Washington, DC: National Association of State Universities and Land-Grant Colleges, 1999), 9.

13. "Auburn University Faculty Handbook: Excerpts Pertaining to Outreach Scholarship, Chapter 3—Section 8-C. Outreach," January 18, 2012, 1, www.auburn.edu/outreach/documents/AU%20Handbook%20Outreach%20Excerpt%20with%20Appendices%201%20&%20A.pdf.

14. CIC Committee on Engagement, "Resource Guide and Recommendations for Defining and Benchmarking Engagement," draft, February 14, 2005, 2, http://apir.wisc.edu/documents/CIC_EngagementReportREV2-22-05.pdf.

15. National Review Board for the Scholarship of Engagement, "Evaluation Criteria for the Scholarship of Engagement," last modified March 2002, www.scholarshipofengagement.org/evaluation/evaluation_criteria.html.

16. Tony Latour, "Building Bridges: The Challenges of a Successful Outreach Program," *Mississippi Libraries* 57 (1993): 103.

Chapter Eight

Professional Development of Liaison Librarians

Fostering Skills for the Twenty-First Century

Gary W. White, **PHD**
Associate Dean for Public Services
University of Maryland Libraries
College Park, MD

Introduction

Professional development encompasses a wide variety of activities and tools and can include formal and informal education, formal and informal learning communities, mentoring and coaching, and individual and group learning, among many other varieties. Jasper states that "anything that you do that contributes to your own knowledge base, understanding and skill can be seen as professional development" and that professional development is on ongoing process that is intertwined with professional practice.[1] Indeed, she argues that it is our professional practice that stimulates the desire to add to our existing knowledge, to seek out new knowledge and skills and to learn from our professional experiences.

As with any profession, ongoing professional development is essential for librarians to keep current with ongoing developments and to develop new skills to meet changing environmental conditions. The *ACRL Statement on Professional Development* (2000) states, "Professional development is an important manifestation of the academic librarian's commitment to personal excellence. It is a necessary response to a rapidly changing environment."[2] Although written over a decade ago, the statement reflects a sentiment that remains true today:

> The strategic position of librarians has never been more promising. Yet the challenges they face are staggering. While the great core of principles, practices and values they espouse remains relevant, the skills and knowledge required to perform their jobs are constantly changing.[3]

The activities and expectations for liaison librarians are evolving and changing at an ever-increasing pace and, according to Laning, Lavallée-Welch and Smith, libraries are one of the most rapidly changing work environments due to advances in technology and a proliferation of information sources.[4] Today, liaison librarians are responsible for a myriad of new roles in teaching, engagement and outreach, scholarly communications, and information technology and in new types of roles in research services and collection development. A recent study shows that, in addition to traditional activities such as collection development and research assistance, new kinds of activities and skills are now expected, including marketing, assessment, data management, project management, partnerships with other campus entities, knowledge and use of institutional repositories, bibliometrics and bibliographic software support, and personnel management, among others.[5] Others discuss the increased focus on relationship building and being proactive.[6]

As this portfolio of required skills and responsibilities grows and changes, the importance of ongoing professional development is apparent. This chapter focuses on best practices for ongoing professional development in the different components of a liaison librarian's responsibilities and includes techniques for assessment of these activities. The first step in ensuring appropriate professional development for each area of responsibility is for each institution to develop a clear list of expected activities for its liaisons. Having a solid understanding of expectations is a necessity for the development of a professional development program. Professional development programs should be developed broadly to include activities for all of the liaisons in a particular institution. In addition, each liaison librarian should work closely with appropriate administrators and mentors to develop an individual plan of professional development for each area of responsibility. The areas covered in this chapter are collections content and access; research services; teaching, learning, and literacies; outreach and engagement; and scholarly communications.

Collections Content and Access

In chapter 5, on collection development, Daniel Mack outlines the major areas of responsibility for collection development as well as assessment and evaluation tools for liaison librarians. Expertise in collection development and management is a skill that continually develops over time. There are a wide variety of activities that will aid in this process, some organizationally driven and others individually driven.

Library administrators can foster professional development for collections-related skills in a number of areas. As mentioned above, library administrators responsible for collections should clearly articulate areas of expectation in this area and offer in-house programs and other resources to support each of these expectations. By emphasizing the importance of these skills, library administrators can encourage or require participation in activities such as regular collections forums or discussions to improve practices. Administration can also support professional development through educational opportunities such as webinars and workshops and through support for participation in other professional venues, such as regional and national conferences. However, successful professional development requires motivation and buy-in from the individual liaison. There must be an environment that encourages and supports this individualized approach to professional development.

Table 8.1 presents a rubric outlining professional development activities that support expectations in this area. Although this table is not comprehensive, it does provide a framework for activities at both organizational and individual levels to support ongoing professional development.

Table 8.1

Professional Development Rubric for Collections Content and Access

Expectation	Organizational Activities	Individual Activities
Meet with collegiate faculty to discuss collections needs	• Provide workshops/forums led by successful liaisons • Provide educational opportunities to enhance subject expertise • Hold meetings between library administration and college deans to discuss needs and strategies for resources • Provide framework for best practices in how to approach/conduct meetings and in how to develop ongoing relationships	• Shadow other liaisons • Seek out mentors who are successful liaisons • Investigate individual faculty research interests • Read college/departmental strategic plans • Investigate departmental websites for news/changes • Keep abreast of curricular changes/ proposals and be proactive in suggesting needed resources • Volunteer to attend departmental meetings • Attend college/departmental functions
Advise the administration on future collections needs	• Provide a framework and schedule for regular communications • Develop best practices for how this information is communicated and shared • Develop standardized procedures that articulate how new resources are acquired	• Set up regular meetings with collections officers • Create a regular/annual collections plan for assigned disciplines • Communicate curricular proposals and changes and related collections needs to collections officers
Participate in the governance of collection development	• Create a model of shared governance for collections that includes opportunities for participation and leadership • Facilitate participation and leadership in workshops/forums	• Investigate how similar subject liaisons at other institutions participate and advocate for their subject areas • Work with supervisor/mentor to participate in these service activities
Create subject-specific collections policies	• Provide framework for creation of policies that clearly articulates format, content, and time line for policies • Create plan for publicizing/ communicating collections policies	• Investigate existing collections policies at other institutions • Work with other liaisons to discuss/ create policies in areas of overlap Consult with faculty to ensure that policies are aligned with curricular and research needs

Table 8.1 ... (Continued)
Professional Development Rubric for Collections Content and Access

Expectation	Organizational Activities	Individual Activities
Develop ongoing assessment program/activates for collections in assigned areas	• Established fiscal calendar for spending • Institute organizational policies and procedures for collections assessment • Incorporate expectations into annual reviews and work plans • Create and conduct training programs for collections assessment	• Regularly survey faculty on research and collections needs • Meet all new faculty to assess collections needs • Monitor new programs and proposals for new programs • Assess collections needs for accreditation reviews • Participate in library-wide reviews of collections • Work with supervisor/mentor to develop individual assessment plan

Research Services

Research services are sometimes described in a broad sense and can include the other areas of responsibility outlined in this chapter and in the other chapters of this book. For our purposes, Craig Gibson and Sarah Murphy in chapter 2 envision research services as "an emerging model of research life-cycle–focused support . . . expanding the traditional repertoire of reference skills and research consultations into a more fully engaged participation, at a programmatic level, across the spectrum of research activities on campus." This conceptualization of research services is somewhat broader than the operational definition of research services currently practiced by many liaisons.

Research services are obviously evolving, and liaisons are involved with many more activities than they may have been in the past. The "expanded repertoire" now includes, according to Jaguszewski and Williams, advanced research support with the disciplines with an emphasis on greater collaboration and interdisciplinary research, where librarians play a key role in connecting researchers to new and unfamiliar disciplines and resources.[7] Liaisons are also working directly with research teams to support needs across the research lifecycle, including information discovery, management, creation and dissemination. Roles in research data management as well as personal information management are new and rapidly expanding areas for most liaisons.

In order to keep up with these rapidly expanding and changing roles, it is imperative that there be investments in a wide range of professional development activities. Table 8.2 provides a framework for institutional and individual professional development activities to support these changing roles in research services. As we see with many emerging areas, it is important for institutions to support new initiatives with specialized resources and personnel, such as the investment in research data management services that has been evident in most large institutions. As these emerging areas of responsibility grow and become more embedded in the fabric of the liaison's work, professional development activities and expertise must expand beyond the scope of one or a few individuals to a level that is of more depth and evident in the skill sets of many or all liaisons.

Table 8.2
Professional Development Rubric for Research Services

Expectation	Organizational Activities	Individual Activities
Understand research and teaching directions for assigned areas	• Provide professional development opportunities • Encourage interaction with disciplinary faculty	• Discuss issues with faculty • Scan and read scholarship in the field • Attend departmental symposia and lectures
Keep abreast of emerging and waning research and teaching interests and develop appropriate strategies	• Encourage and support continuing education • Support participation in college and department activities • Provide forums for sharing new developments and gaining skills	• Monitor and read professional literature of the disciplines • Participate in departmental activities • Meet with faculty and students individually to understand research needs
Identify key personnel in academic departments/colleges and contact/communicate with them	• Build expectations into work plans • Offer guidelines and best practices	• Set up schedule of meeting regularly with faculty and program directors • Meet with new faculty and others soon after their arrival

Table 8.2 ... (Continued)
Professional Development Rubric for Research Services

Expectation	Organizational Activities	Individual Activities
Participate in the academic operations of the department/ college and assigned communities	• Provide flexibility and expectations for participation • Support communities of practice	• Contact departmental and college administrative support personnel • Work with department heads and program directors • Attend meetings and events
Identify potential donors and work with development personnel	• Provide training and workshops on development activities • Require liaisons to identify development opportunities and participate in development activities	• Regularly identify and communicate potential development opportunities • Meet with development office regularly • Connect potential donors with development office
Identify key vendors and publishers and actively cultivate relationships	• Provide coordinated approach to vendor relationships • Support best practices and offer centralized support • Support consortial efforts	• Monitor publishing trends and issues • Work with peers in subject discipline to identify issues and resolve problems • Discuss issues with vendors at conferences • Communicate vendor issues/ problems to collections/ acquisitions personnel
Identify potential areas of partnership between libraries and communities	• Support culture of outreach • Encourage administration and librarians to be proactive and to initiate meetings to explore partnerships	• Be proactive • Discuss potential ideas with department head and other administrators • Set up meetings with relevant campus and community members to discuss how the library can support their efforts
Develop individualized program of assessment for outreach and engagement	• Provide coordinated approach to assessment • Offer assistance and training for assessment	• Set goals for outreach and engagement and regularly monitor • Assess individual activities and engage in program of continuous improvement • Review activities periodically throughout the year

Teaching, Learning, and Literacies

Ellysa Stern Cahoy and Maria Barefoot, in chapters 3 and 4, focus on assessing a liaison librarian's instructional programs and initiatives, including those related to online and blended learning. Liaison librarians have traditionally been active in providing course-related instruction as well as participating in more general types of library instructional activities. However, as the importance of information literacy is more broadly recognized, liaison librarians are adopting new roles and activities in teaching and learning.

Jaguszewski and Williams discuss the expanding roles for liaisons in support of teaching and learning.[8] While the importance of librarians in supporting teaching and learning is recognized, there are difficulties in scaling this support broadly. There are also organizational and institutional constraints on new approaches and tools, such as models for embedded librarianship and for the development of online learning modules and other online tools. In addition, Jaguszewski and Williams describe how the concept of information literacy is being expanded to include areas such as media, visual, and data literacy. As Cahoy and Barefoot both discuss, it is vital for liaisons to engage in these new models and to employ assessment techniques that demonstrate the liaison's impact on learning and on developing information literacy skills.

Cahoy and Barefoot both offer frameworks for the assessment of teaching, literacies, and learning. For both authors, institutional support and the creation of a culture of assessment are vital components for an effective liaison program in these areas. Table 8.3 presents a rubric similar to those for collections content and access and for research services by providing a number of suggested organizational and individual activities that can help meet the existing and emerging expectations for teaching, literacies, and learning.

Table 8.3
Professional Development Rubric for Teaching, Learning, and Literacies

Expectation	Organizational Activities	Individual Activities
Provide effective, responsive research/reference services via all media: telephone, chat, IM, social media	• Provide training programs, discussion forums, and avenues to share best practices	• Actively seek out ways to improve services • Work with peers or mentors to develop plan for skill acquisition and improvement
Offer individual research consultations/office hours	• Integrate into work plan/overall workload • Training for best practices	• Schedule, plan, and promote availability • Be proactive and visible to assigned departments • Create goal of meeting with each faculty member at least once per year
Possess excellent customer service skills: civility, respect for diversity, approachability, timely responses/timely follow-up	• Create customer service training program with expectations and method of assessment	• Proactively seek to improve skills • Develop good time management skills • Elicit feedback and other assessments
Provide written/electronic reference guides	• Create standards for guides • Provide infrastructure for creation, maintenance, and support	• Develop plan for creating and updating guides on a regular basis • Stay up-to-date on resources and tools available • Consult with peers and professional colleagues on best practices
Monitor and understand changes in the production of knowledge in subject disciplines as well as in general	• Encourage and support continuing education • Support participation in college and department activities • Provide forums for sharing new developments and gaining skills	• Monitor and read professional literature of the disciplines • Participate in department activities • Meet with faculty and students individually to understand research needs
Gather, document, and analyze data; conduct ongoing assessment of services	• Create framework for gathering and documenting data • Provide central support for methods of assessment	• Work with administration and mentor to develop plan of assessment • Develop plan for gathering and documenting activities and do so consistently

Outreach and Engagement

As Marcy Bidney describes in chapter 7, outreach and engagement are two activities that permeate all aspects of librarianship. Outreach and engagement activities are vital for libraries and librarians to develop future-centered service models, to bring users in, to facilitate knowledge creation, and to promote innovative ways to use library collections. Jaguszewski and Williams likewise argue that engagement is critical for liaisons:

> Research libraries are now compelled to understand and support all processes of instruction and scholarship, which calls for an engagement model. An engaged liaison seeks to enhance scholarly productivity, to empower learners, and to participate in the entire lifecycle of the research, teaching and learning process. Engagement requires an outward focus. By understanding the changing needs and practices of scholars and students, librarians can help shape the future directions for the library and advance the library's mission within the larger institution. Building strong relationships with faculty and other campus professionals, and establishing collaborative partnerships within and across institutions, are necessary building blocks to librarians' success.[9]

As with the tables presented earlier, table 8.4 outlines both organizational and individual activities that can be used to meet expectations for outreach and engagement.

Table 8.4
Professional Development Rubric for Outreach and Engagement

Expectation	Organizational Activities	Individual Activities
Educate and inform faculty and students about relevant issues	• Develop expertise through scholarly communications program • Offer training programs for liaisons • Publicize activities and information to campus community • Work with campus leaders on relevant issues	• Participate in educational and training activities • Discuss best practices for communicating and working with faculty • Include information on scholarly communications in orientation and other programs

Table 8.4 ... (Continued)
Professional Development Rubric for Outreach and Engagement

Expectation	Organizational Activities	Individual Activities
Advocate for sustainable models of scholarly communication	• Provide campus leadership in scholarly communications issues • Provide framework and training for individual librarians	• Communicate regularly with college and departments about library-wide efforts as well as national trends • Seek ways to advance efforts
Work closely with faculty and students to understand their workflows and patterns of scholarly communications	• Provide high-level training and resources for gathering and analyzing information	• Develop regular schedule and tools for systematically gathering and analyzing information
Develop tools and services to facilitate scholarly communications	• Provide centralized support for gathering information and for offering services • Create centralized Web presence and other tools	• Work with library leaders and national experts to develop discipline-specific tools and services
Develop expertise in copyright, data curation, and open-access issues that are relevant to subject areas	• Create or hire copyright/data curation/open access specialist(s) • Provide broad training on relevant issues • Develop centralized Web presence for tools and info	• Seek out training and skills related to copyright, data curation, and open access • Understand relevant issues related to one's discipline and for various formats
Develop knowledge or expertise in research data management	• Hire or train librarians in this area • Develop training and workshops	• Seek out training and skills related to RDM • Understand important RDM issues related to one's discipline and for various formats
Support and promote use of institutional repositories	• Promote repositories at institutional and national level • Support use by librarians • Provide easy ingest and retrieval • Support various formats and functions • Support development and maintenance of repository	• Develop expertise in using • Deposit one's own works • Integrate into orientations, activities, webpages, and outreach materials
Help design and implement online tools and services to meet the needs of discipline/interdisciplinary research communities	• Conduct needs assessment • Work with campus research offices and research administration to develop priorities and plan	• Work with disciplinary research centers • Conduct needs assessment

Table 8.4 ... (Continued)
Professional Development Rubric for Outreach and Engagement

Expectation	Organizational Activities	Individual Activities
Document and share practices	• Develop and promote tool kits, forums, and workshops • Support professional development activities outside institution	• Incorporate into work plans and review documents • Share best practices with disciplinary peers
Assess individual programs and participate in broader assessment programs that include both qualitative and quantitative components	• Provide framework for assessment • Establish guiding principles and expected practices • Provide training in assessment tools	• Develop individual plan of assessment and incorporate items into work plans • Obtain skills in qualitative and quantitative assessment techniques • Participate in institutional assessment programs

Scholarly Communications

While liaison roles are rapidly changing in all areas of responsibility, activities associated with scholarly communications are perhaps the newest and most daunting for liaison librarians. As Dawn Childress and Daniel Hickey discuss in chapter 6, areas of emerging focus are data curation, open access, library-supported publishing models, and digital scholarship, as well as more traditional areas such as copyright and author rights.

From a professional development standpoint, scholarly communications activities are challenging because they encompass a wide range of activities. As these are newer areas of responsibility, libraries have largely attempted to address the needs for support via specialized training of a few, or just one, librarian. As demand grows for these services, the need for broader-based expertise and training is critical. While the current model of referrals and consultations can address limited and short-term needs, as these activities become more integrated and are expected services, liaisons will need to develop more in-depth knowledge and skills to support these demands.

Jaguszewski and Williams, in their study of emerging roles for liaisons in research libraries, note that liaisons are now expected to have general knowledge of copyright and intellectual property issues, but that institutions also need to have resident experts in these areas.[10] As liaisons become more involved with online learning and MOOCs, knowledge and expertise in copyright, authors' rights, and other open-access issues becomes increasingly important. Jaguszewski and Williams discuss the growing pressure for researchers to plan and manage their own scholarly output and the trend toward more acceptance of open-access publishing models as drivers for liaisons to become more engaged in these areas.

Childress and Hickey provide a framework for assessment that includes both quantitative and qualitative assessment strategies and techniques. As with other areas covered in this book, Childress and Hickey discuss the need for assessment at both the individual and organizational levels. Table 8.5 is a rubric providing suggested expectations for liaisons in the area of scholarly communications. The table includes professional development activities that individuals can pursue as well as those that can be offered by the organization. As with the other areas covered in this chapter, there is no single path to success in developing a professional development program in scholarly communications. Rather, it is a function and combination of organizational expectations and support as well as individual motivation and need.

Table 8.5
Professional Development Rubric for Scholarly Communications

Expectation	Organizational Activities	Individual Activities
Educate and inform students and faculty about available information resources and research tools and how to use them	• Communicate and share new resources and tools	• Keep abreast of new collections • Work with peers locally and nationally
Collaborate in the design, implementation, and maintenance of online tools and services that meet the needs of users	• Provide training and assistance in development of online tools • Share best practices	• Actively develop needed skills and keep abreast of new technologies and tools

Table 8.5 ... (Continued)
Professional Development Rubric for Scholarly Communications

Expectation	Organizational Activities	Individual Activities
Proactively establish partnerships with teaching faculty and researchers	• Incorporate expectations into individual work plans • Establish partnerships and build relationships at organizational level	• Set up individual meetings on a regular basis • Meet all new faculty • Develop research and interest profile for each
Become more active participants in courses; move away from single sessions	• Provide support for use of online tools for general tutorials • Provide resources and time for librarians to become embedded • Provide training and support for blended learning and flipped classroom approaches	• Partner with faculty to develop objectives and assessment tools for information literacy • Seek integration into courses via course management systems
Conduct needs assessment; understand needs of community of users	• Provide centralized support and training for conducting needs assessments/surveys • Develop best practices	• Partner with peers and faculty to develop appropriate tools • Analyze national trends • Develop schedule of assessment activities
Understand research and scholarly communication patterns of disciplines	• Provide professional development opportunities • Encourage interaction with disciplinary faculty	• Discuss issues with faculty • Scan and read scholarship in the field • Attend departmental symposia and lectures
Teach in subject-specific and general curriculum courses	• Provide framework for teaching expectations • Provide resources, spaces, and technology to enable teaching to occur in a variety of formats/spaces	• Actively seek out opportunities • Work with program coordinators and department heads • Engage new faculty in opportunities • Offer variety of possible ways to teach
Develop and implement innovative instructional design approaches and formats	• Support training and professional development in instruction for librarians • Offer workshops and forums • Provide technologies and tools	• Participate in professional development activities related to teaching • Proactively seek out innovative techniques and tools
Develop skills via conferences, seminars, and professional development activities	• Provide centralized funding and expectations for participation • Develop internal program of professional development • Hire those with needed skills	• Devote professional development time and energy to teaching • Participate in organizational programs • Seek out free resources and communities of practice

Table 8.5 ...(Continued)
Professional Development Rubric for Scholarly Communications

Expectation	Organizational Activities	Individual Activities
Develop appropriate qualitative and quantitative assessment methods that evaluate impact on student performance and retention	• Provide centralized training and support for assessment activities • Offer workshops and forums for skill development • Develop techniques and mechanisms for reporting to institution	• Seek out necessary training • Develop best practices along with community of peers • Participate in organizational activities
Acquire and use feedback from students and faculty	• Develop organization-wide tools for obtaining feedback • Collect and analyze feedback for the organization as a whole and for individuals	• Develop specific tools and techniques for gathering regular feedback • Seek alternative methods targeting different populations • Develop communications plan for how feedback is being used
Participate in a culture of quality by continuously evaluating and adjusting instructional methods	• Provide centralized tools for evaluation and easy mechanisms, tools, and spaces to adjust instruction • Encourage innovation and experimentation and sharing of best practices	• Work with peers and colleagues to develop innovative approaches • Experiment with new approaches and evaluate outcomes
Proactively explore new opportunities for teaching	• Place a value on teaching; facilitate opportunities • Provide necessary resources (time, equipment, space, support) for teaching	• Discuss options and opportunities with individual faculty • Share possible ways of integrating library instruction into course content • Seek out participation in new courses
Understand and participate in course management systems	• Partner with centralized IT to ensure library integration • Build tools and programs to ensure easy integration of librarians and library resources	• Actively develop needed skills and keep abreast of new technologies and tools • Seek out necessary training • Seek integration into courses via course management systems
Keep abreast of learning trends, including in-person, blended, and online	• Provide centralized training, workshops, forums, webinars • Support professional development of instructional librarians • Connect with campus leaders in teaching and learning	• Regularly read the higher education and library literature • Participate in professional programs and activities • Monitor campus activities regarding teaching and learning

Conclusion

An effective program of professional development requires a diversity of activities and resources at both the organizational and individual levels. Organizations must create an environment in which professional development is expected and supported, and they must offer programs and activities to meet the wide-ranging needs of liaison librarians. Individuals must also take personal responsibility for their own professional development. In fact, personal motivation is key for success in the area of professional development. Issues for individuals and organizations to consider are how to develop programs that are timely and relevant. For the individual, selecting from a seemingly endless array of possibilities can be daunting.

This chapter offers a framework for developing a program of organizational and individual professional development activities by organizing possibilities based on existing and emerging expectations for liaison librarians. The areas of responsibility covered in this chapter are not mutually exclusive. Rather, they overlap in scope and are interrelated but share a common theme: they all necessitate a close working relationship with faculty and an integration with the research and teaching processes. As roles and activities develop and grow in demand, liaisons must proactively engage in necessary professional development activities, and institutions must provide the resources and capacity to support these needs. Jaguszewski and Williams acknowledge that libraries and librarians are grappling with these new roles, and challenges exist in identifying these new roles, determining what existing activities can diminish or cease, creating supportive institutional structures, and ensuring that liaisons have the needed skills and knowledge.[11] The areas covered in this chapter and the suggested framework for institutional and individual activities for professional development provide a roadmap to help libraries and liaisons to navigate these new demands.

Notes

1. Melanie Jasper, *Reflection, Decision-Making and Professional Development,* Vital Notes for Nurses (Oxford: Blackwell Publishing, 2006), 21-22.

2. ACRL Professional Development Committee, *ACRL Statement on Professional Development* (Chicago: Association of College and Research Libraries, 2000), www.ala.org/acrl/publications/whitepapers/acrlstatement.

3. Ibid.

4. Melissa Laning, Catherine Lavallée-Welch, and Margo Smith, "Frontiers of Effort: Librarians and Professional Development Blogs," *Journal of Library Administration* 43, no. 3/4 (2005): 161–179, doi:10.1300/J111v43n03_13.

5. Antony Brewerton, "'…And Any Other Duties Deemed Necessary': An Analysis of Subject Librarian Job Descriptions," *SCONUL Focus,* no. 51 (2011): 60–67, www.sconul.ac.uk/sites/default/files/documents/18_2.pdf.

6. Stephen Pinfield, "The Changing Role of Subject Librarians in Academic Libraries," *Journal of Librarianship and Information Science* 33, no. 1 (March 2001): 32–38; Kara Whatley, "New Roles of Liaison Librarians: A Liaison's Perspective," in *Research Library Issues* no. 265, Special Issue on Liaison Librarian Roles (August 2009): 29–32, http://publications.arl.org/rli265.

7. Janice M. Jaguszewski and Karen Williams, *New Roles for New Times: Transforming Liaison Roles in Research Libraries* (Washington, DC: Association of Research Libraries, 2013).

8. Ibid.

9. Ibid., 4.

10. Jaguszewski and Williams, *New Roles for New Times.*

11. Ibid.

Conclusion

Designing and Implementing a Liaison Assessment Program

Daniel C. Mack
Associate Dean for Collection Strategies and Services
University of Maryland Libraries
College Park, MD

The preceding authors have presented a variety of tools for assessing the work for which liaison librarians are responsible in the contemporary academic library. The task now facing the librarian or library supervisor is how to incorporate this information into a functioning liaison assessment program. This undertaking consists of two phases: first designing, and then implementing, an assessment program. Both phases require participation and buy-in from throughout the organization, particularly from the liaison librarians themselves, from their supervisors, and from the top level of the library administration.

Designing a liaison librarian assessment program can be a daunting task. The single best advice is to start small, and start immediately. A library can assess virtually any activity or program, but this does not mean that it should do so. Rather, the library should begin by identifying a reasonable number of activities to assess, perhaps even starting with a single service or program. Depending on the mission and goals of the library and the institution it serves, an initial assessment program could focus on liaison services related to reference and research assistance, library instruction, collection development, scholarly communication, or some other type of engagement and outreach. After targeting specific areas in which to conduct assessment, the next decision is to decide whom to assess and how to conduct assessment. This involves identifying assessment measures and tools that the library can implement.

Next, the library should create a time line for assessment activities. Will assessment be ongoing, or will the library conduct it at specific times? The answer to this question may vary depending on the activity or service that is being assessed. For example, it often makes sense to conduct assessment of library instruction during those times of the academic year in which liaison librarians perform such instruction. On the other hand, some collection development activities are closely tied to a budget calendar, and the library might best link assessment of these activities to the fiscal cycle. Still other liaison efforts, such as reference and research services and other types of engagement and outreach, might be more or less ongoing, and assessment of these services might best be ongoing. What makes sense for one library, or even one librarian, could very well be inappropriate for another. The development of an assessment program must therefore not only take into account differences of activities, but also when is the best time to accomplish the task.

Perhaps the most important part of a liaison assessment program is how the library incorporates the results of assessment into the professional development of individual librarians as well as modification of its overall services. Individual assessment should be linked closely to librarians' work plans and annual reviews. Likewise, assessment of both individual personnel as well as of larger library services and programs must inform strategic planning at the departmental and library-wide level. This requires collective buy-in from across the library. It is necessary that those librarians participating in assessment understand the program's importance and process, as well as how assessment will improve their work. The library administration must also make a strong commitment to support the assessment program. This requires that the administration ensure that all personnel are given the opportunity for input into the program as well as the necessary information, training, and support to conduct assessment. The administration must also clearly articulate expectations and outcomes of the assessment program.

An important component of a programmatic approach to assessment of liaison activities and services is how the assessment program will affect not only the library but also the larger institution that the library serves. Wilson compares the role of liaison librarians to that of consultants in the business world.[1] By demonstrating how librarians can facilitate the work of the academic departments, faculty, students, and subject areas for which they are responsible, the library can employ assessment to demonstrate its continued importance to the intellectual life of the academy. Part of this also includes reporting the results of assessment to university administrators, consortial partners, donors and other funding sources, and other stakeholders. Both quantitative and qualitative assessment efforts can lead to the creation of powerful narratives about how library liaison activities benefit the university at large. For example, Nutefall and Gaspar tell how assessment of their instruction program provided their library with the documentation that the library needed to show the positive impact that this instruction had on student success.[2] As a result, their library received two additional positions from their university. An assessment program should therefore identify specific audiences and means of communication for reporting positive outcomes.

To create and implement an ongoing assessment program the library must take specific actions and collaborate with a variety of persons and groups. In summary, the library should create a plan for implementing these steps:

- **Target programs or activities to assess.** These should be central to the vision, mission, and goals of both the library and the larger institution that it supports.
- **Identify persons to participate in assessment.** This will include liaison librarians who deliver the services and programs under assessment. It may also involve their supervisors, as well as

support staff, personnel responsible for training and professional development, and others within the library.

- **Communicate about the assessment program widely throughout the library.** Because assessment involves many people across the organization and at every level, the success of an assessment program requires wide-scale cooperation and buy-in.

- **Identify relevant assessment tools, measures, and practices relevant to the programs or services that the library plans to assess.** The chapters of this book offer information about a wide range of assessment tools that libraries and liaisons can adopt, adapt, and incorporate into their own programs.

- **Establish a timetable for assessment.** Setting deadlines that are reasonable for the services under assessment can greatly facilitate the library's efforts to implement and conduct the program.

- **Provide personnel with training and support for conducting assessment.** While some assessment activities might seem straightforward, others are more complex. The library administration must ensure that individual librarians have the preparation and backing they need to participate in assessment.

- **Report on results of assessment both internally and externally.** Within the library, assessment outcomes can create community by developing collective pride in accomplishments, as well as shared responsibility for improving services. By presenting positive assessment outcomes to university administrators, academic departments, funders, and other stakeholders, the library can demonstrate the constructive impact that its liaisons have within the academy.

- **Incorporate assessment into professional development, annual reviews, modification of existing library programs, and creation of new services.** A major goal of assessment is to create a climate of continuous service improvement. Ultimately, a liaison assessment program will provide the library with well-trained librarians, a suite of services and programs that are relevant to the institution it serves, and an ongoing cycle of examination, communication, training, and improvement.

Higher education will continue to give assessment a significant place in its activities. Likewise, the work that liaison librarians perform will remain central as the primary interface between the library and the institution it serves. Assessment gives the library the means by which it can institute improvements, develop its personnel, and document the positive impact it has on its users. By designing and implementing a robust program of assessment for liaison librarians, the twenty-first-century academic library can continue to offer services that are relevant to the university's curriculum and research enterprise.

Notes

1.   E. Michael Wilson, "The Role of Library Liaison as Consultant," *Kentucky Libraries* 77, no. 1 (Winter 2013): 14–19.

2.   Jennifer E. Nutefall and Deborah Gaspar, "Raise Your Profile: Build Your Program," *Public Services Quarterly* 4, no. 2 (2008): 127–135, doi:10.1080/15228950802202432.

About the Authors

Maria R. Barefoot is the Health Sciences Librarian at Youngstown State University. Her subject specialties include nursing, physical therapy, health professions, human performance and exercise science, and human ecology. She has published previously in *MLA News*.

Marcy Bidney has been Curator of the American Geographical Society Library since October 2012. Bidney's professional affiliations include the American Library Association, where she has chaired several committees and discussion groups and served as chair of the Map and Geospatial Information Roundtable in 2011. She served on the Cartographic Users Advisory Counsel, with the International Federation of Library Associations on the Government Information and Official Publications Committee as secretary, and is a member of the Association of American Geographers Archives and Association History Committee. Bidney's main interest and research focus in libraries includes utilizing evolving technologies to provide increased access to geographic information collections in libraries, a topic on which she has published a number of articles. Other interests include the digital and spatial humanities, geographic education, the history of cartography, and the history of geography.

Ellysa Stern Cahoy is an Education Librarian and the Assistant Director of the Pennsylvania Center for the Book in the Penn State University Libraries, University Park. A former children's librarian and school library media specialist, Cahoy has published research and presented on information literacy, evidence-based librarianship, library instruction, and personal archiving. In 2012, she was awarded a $143,000 grant from the Andrew W. Mellon Foundation to fund the exploration of faculty's personal scholarly archiving practices and needs. Cahoy is past chair of the Association of College and Research Libraries (ACRL) Information

Literacy Competency Standards Committee and chaired the initial ACRL Information Literacy Competency Standards Review Task Force. In 2013, Cahoy received the Miriam Dudley Instruction Librarian Award from the ACRL Instruction Section.

Dawn Childress is Humanities Librarian and the Kalin Librarian for Technological Innovation at Penn State Libraries, where she serves as liaison to the departments of German and Slavic languages and literatures, French and Francophone studies, comparative literature, and philosophy. She also regularly consults and collaborates with researchers on projects related to digital scholarship and pedagogy, scholarly communication, and publishing. Her background is in German literature, philosophy, book history, and textual studies.

Craig Gibson is Professor and Head of the FAES (Food, Agriculture, and Environmental Science) Library at the Ohio State University. He has also been Associate Director for Research and Education at Ohio State, with responsibilities for reference and research services, outreach and engagement, the libraries' instruction program, and departmental libraries. Previously, he was Associate University Librarian for Research, Instruction, and Outreach at George Mason University Libraries and has held other positions in instruction and reference services at Washington State University and Lewis-Clark State College. His current research interests focus on threshold concepts for information literacy, research and learning commons and their relation to student success, and engagement measures for academic and research libraries. He has taught in the ACRL Immersion Program since 2000, has been editor of the ACRL Publications in Librarianship series since 2008, and is currently co-chair of the ACRL Information Literacy Standards Revision Task Force.

Daniel Hickey is the Assistant Director of the Hospitality, Labor, and Management Library at Cornell University. Hickey graduated from the University of Pittsburgh's School of Information Sciences in 2009. While studying in Pittsburgh, he helped create metadata for Warhol's *Time Capsules*, a work of art composed of a large, uncatalogued collection of Andy Warhol's personal effects. Hickey has published on virtual research support services and copyright and fair use; he blogs at http://danhickey. tumblr.com.

Daniel C. Mack is Associate Dean for Collection Strategies and Services at the University of Maryland Libraries in College Park, where he provides leadership in policy creation and implementation, strategic planning, program development, and assessment for library collections. His previous positions include Tombros Librarian for Classics and Ancient Mediterranean Studies, Professor of Classics and the Bibliography of Antiquity, and Head of the George and Sherry Middlemas Arts and Humanities Library at Penn State and Library Director at the Dauphin County (PA) Prison. An active member of the American Library Association, Mack was recently appointed to ALA's Committee on Library Advocacy. He holds advanced degrees in library science and ancient history and has taught college courses in ancient history, Roman archaeology, classical literature, Latin grammar, and library research methods. Recent publications include work as co-editor of the Association of College and Research Libraries' monograph *Interdisciplinarity and Academic Libraries* and as consulting editor for *Brill's New Pauly: Encyclopaedia of the Ancient World.* Mack's current research interests include interdisciplinarity in the twenty-first-century academy, assessment of library collections and services, and Roman civilization in the age of Caesar Augustus.

Sarah Anne Murphy is current Coordinator of Assessment for the Ohio State University Libraries. She earned a master of library science from Kent State University in 2000 and a master in business administration from the Ohio State University, Fisher College of Business, in 2008. Murphy edited *The Quality Infrastructure: Measuring, Analyzing, and Improving Library Services* (Chicago: ALA Editions, 2013) and authored *The Librarian as Information Consultant: Transforming Reference for* *the Information Age* (Chicago: ALA Editions, 2011). She has published several papers on library assessment, Lean Six Sigma, mentoring, and veterinary medicine libraries in *College and Research Libraries,* the *Journal of Academic Librarianship,* and the *Journal of the Medical Library Association.*

Gary W. White is Associate Dean for Public Services in the University Libraries at the University of Maryland. White has responsibility for library research and teaching services to the university as well as oversight of all subject libraries. He has a PhD in higher education, a master of business administration, and a master of library science and is also a member of the university's blended and online learning commission. White has over twenty years of professional experience as an academic librarian and administrator, with numerous books, refereed journal articles, and scholarly presentations.

Index